PRAISE FOR

Still

STANDING

D1455883

"Still Standing" is an empowering read from one of the most inspiring individuals our agency has had the privilege of working with. Dwight Owens has taken a misfortune that occurred in his life and embraced it to inspire and touch so many lives. He has been a true advocate for individuals with disabilities and for the work of our agency. After reading this book, I can promise you it will touch your heart and inspire you to be the best version of yourself. I encourage everyone to read "Still Standing!"

Chris Howard, Executive Director
Mississippi Department of Rehabilitation Services

"Life is a gift; sometimes the gift wrap tears and the bow unravels. Hope, though, never dies. Let Dwight Owens inspire you as he continues to rewrap his gift of life and presents it to others."

Evelyn Kormanik, Founder
Staten Island (NY) Giving Circle

"This is the best first-person account of the rehab process I have ever read."

Chris Blount, Executive Director
Wilson Research Foundation at Methodist Rehabilitation Center

"I plan to have every person in my office read this book."

Dr. Duncan Donald, Trauma Medical Director
Forrest General Hospital

Still STANDING

BY
DWIGHT OWENS
JONATHAN W. PRAET

TABLE OF CONTENTS

PROLOGUE

"That guy is driving way too fast," I said out loud to myself. In the rearview mirror, I could see a big Chevy truck speeding up behind me, its driver seemingly unconcerned by the pounding rain. "He'll probably just pass me," I thought, and I turned my attention back to the road ahead.

BAM! The Chevy slammed into the rear of my car, and both vehicles immediately swerved out of control—mine into the steep gully off Highway 84, where it stopped instantly upon impact with a tree; his ending up in a ditch on the other side of the road. I immediately passed out but regained consciousness just long enough to feel blood streaming from my mouth. I had time only to whisper a prayer before passing out again. "Please save me, God."

Life can turn on a dime, and mine did just that in a matter of seconds. It would be days before my family and I learned the damage: six broken ribs, punctured lungs, my liver lodged in my chest cavity, my back fractured in several places, and a severed spinal cord. I coded twice shortly after the accident, and the doctors were ready to call my death. But I came back… against all odds. Why?

We didn't know for days whether I would survive or what kind of life I could have if I did. I didn't learn for a week that I would be paralyzed forever from the waist down.

My name is Dwight Owens. This is my story.

Dwight Owens
December 2011

A NOTE FROM THE AUTHOR

We all need an occasional dollop of inspiration, and I got mine in full measure by speaking with Dwight several times a week for the better part of a year. He had numerous physical setbacks along the way, which slowed progress on his story. His enthusiasm never waned, however, and he was always ready for the next phase.

"What's next? I can't wait," he said time and again.

The pressure was on. I needed my prose to match Dwight's spirit, and it was no easy task. Dwight's enthusiasm and high spirits were infectious, and they always made me look at my own small disability as nothing more than a bump in the road of life. After all, if Dwight can smile and inspire people every day, the least I could do was not complain.

I have severe eye degradation resulting from a condition called wet macular degeneration. My vision is blurred and splotchy all the time, and it makes it difficult to clatter away on the computer and read what I'm writing. Some days are better than others, but every day was a good day when I got my prescription refilled with a dose of Dwight's spirit.

Just as Dwight's character is an inspiration to me, I hope his story will inspire many others. He found the courage to press on against long odds. He endured unspeakable pain. And he came out of the tunnel a stronger, wiser man. He brings hope to the hopeless, and he makes life better for the people who fill the world around him. Dwight lives the message he preaches, and his favorite phrase is "I can do it." He's shown me that he can.

Jonathan W. Praet
December 2011

1

A DEATH IN THE FAMILY

I was getting ready for school with my two brothers and sister when we got a call from our Grandmother Venice. Cedrick, my older brother, picked up the phone.

"Cedrick," Grandmother Venice said, "tell the other kids your Dad's been hit by a car outside MacDonald's Store. I think he's okay. Get on the bus and go to school. I'll fill you in when you get back this afternoon."

We soon learned she had never been more wrong. Dad had been shot and was at that very moment struggling for his life. The day was Monday, December 14, 1994.

MacDonald's Store was one of only two stores in the small town of Hot Coffee, Mississippi, where I grew up, and we passed it every day on the way to school. On this particular day, we piled into the bus and sat together in the front seats. Usually we split up as soon as we got on and sat in different sections, but after what our grandmother had told us, we wanted to get a good look when the bus got to MacDonald's. We were surprised to see a fleet of police cars and a large crowd of people on the side of the road as we approached. Cedrick yelled at the bus driver to stop and let us off. He did, and the scene that unfolded before us has lived in my memory ever since.

A man's body was sprawled out on the side of the road with a huge stream of blood running from his head toward the gully a few feet away. Brain matter was sprayed in an arc around his head and there was a gaping hole where his skull should have been. His eyes were open, and they fixed on the four of us.

"Dad?" I whispered. His lips were quivering as he tried to say something to us. Then his body froze, and he went completely still. The image of my Dad lying in a pool of blood in the street is engraved forever in my mind, and I can picture him as vividly today as when it occurred seventeen years ago. He was thirty-three years old.

Mom had received a call at work and had arrived at the scene just minutes before us. She was sobbing so uncontrollably she didn't see us get off the bus. Every so often, she would raise her head to look at Dad, then immediately look down again. An onlooker told her we were there, and she gained enough presence of mind to let her maternal instinct take over. She wrapped her arms around her brood and herded us off to the side.

"Your Dad was shot," she tried to explain through her tears. "We don't know who did it or why. A car drove by about fifteen minutes ago and somebody shoved him out the door. That's all we know." She said this between sobs, and she gasped for breath with each word. My sister Aletha started crying because Mom was crying, and Mom just hugged her as close as she could. The three of us boys, Cedrick, Voncarie, and I, stood there silent and wide-eyed among all the people and cars. We were dazed and didn't know what to do or how to respond.

We stayed there for a few minutes longer, and I watched as the EMTs placed my Dad into a body bag. They struggled with the zipper for a moment—I remember this striking me as insulting and somehow undignified. Then they lifted him matter-or-factly into the ambulance and drove off, leaving a large pool of blood on the side of the road that would remain visible for the next three weeks. The police had secured the area and were questioning onlookers and people in nearby houses. Several small pockets of people remained at the scene as we left, crying and hugging each other.

Our house was already filled with people when we got home. Grandmother Venice was distraught. She was always the strong one, the person who could deal with anything and never lose her composure, and I was stunned to see her sobbing. My sister was still crying, and Mom broke down again. Neighbors and friends were arriving every few minutes to do what they could. They brought coffee, food, and condolences. Mostly they just sat with us and shared our grief.

I tried to make myself invisible and take in the scene as best I could. It was all unreal to me, like a dream. All at once, I was overwhelmed by the need to be alone. I went to my room and locked the door, and the moment I did, tears overtook me, and I couldn't contain them. Dad had always been so strong, so manly, so invincible. He prided himself on his physical strength; he was built like a professional athlete. How could this have happened to him? What did it mean? What were we going to do? I sobbed and sobbed, but I didn't want anybody to see me. Dad had always taught us to be strong no matter the circumstances. Whenever I scraped a knee or hit my thumb with a hammer, he would say, "Tough it out, Dwight. You can handle it." But he had always meant this in terms of physical pain, not emotional pain. Nothing he had taught me could have prepared me for this.

Dad had his share of flaws, but he was a loving, attentive father. He was quick with a smile, and he was not afraid to say he loved us. He said it all the time, and we knew he meant it. That day, alone in my room, I felt a cold void open in my heart that could never be sealed again.

I thought of the time a few months before when Cedrick and I had taken a hike with him in the nearby woods. Cedrick was in eighth grade, and I was in sixth. Our younger brother Voncarie was only in third grade, so he had not come along with us. Dad carried a small wood saw with him and took us to a place he had already chosen ahead of time. When we arrived, we spent the next hour carving the words "Tree Cedrick" and "Tree Dwight" into two large trees standing side by side.

As we worked, Dad explained, "Boys, you two are like these trees. You will grow tall and strong and be able to withstand anything. No matter what, you'll still be standing when the dust clears. And these are brother trees. They see the world together, they share their experiences, and they protect each other from the wind and rain. This is Tree Cedrick, and this is Tree Dwight. I want you two to be strong and true to each other just like these trees for all your lives." Although Cedrick and I have many loving memories of our Dad, this is our favorite.

Our Dad's murder dominated local news coverage and was the talk of the surrounding towns for the next month. As I think back on it now, I realize it broke my heart to hear newscasters focusing on Dad's flaws instead of his many virtues. They never talked about how much he loved his children and how much we loved him. They never talked about how hard he worked as a lumberman or how he was admired as a true and loyal friend by the people close to him. Those details, however true, weren't salacious enough, so instead, the news media spiced up the story by focusing on how Mom and Dad had gotten married when she was only sixteen and he eighteen and how they had separated and gotten back together several times before finally divorcing. Dad was very casual about fidelity, and although he loved Mom, his infidelities had finally led to their divorce. That was hard on the family, and it was harder yet to hear about it on the news every day. They never mentioned that Dad was still around all the time, was a loving father to his children, and met all his commitments to the family. They never talked about that.

We watched the news coverage of Dad's death every day that week, and we grew angrier and angrier at the litany of Dad's shortcomings. The real message seemed to be: "Well, what else would you expect from a family like this?"

And as if that weren't enough, the news coverage also fanned the flames of racial tension and fear in our community. Dad had committed the one sin that was unforgivable at that time in Southern Mississippi: he was dating a white woman when he was shot. Rumors were flying, and the news reports continually speculated that this relationship might have prompted his tragic murder. Reporters always mentioned this detail in grave tones, as if it could somehow ignite race riots across the land. "Was this a revenge killing by an old boyfriend of the white woman?" they wondered. Dad's body had been dumped in the closest thing Hot Coffee had to a town center, as if the killer were trying to send a message. "What was that message? Was this a warning for others?" the reports speculated. They wanted ratings, and the best way to get them was to sully my father's character and stoke the fears of the community.

We took off from school for the remainder of the week—a singular event in our home. Mom and Dad always insisted we go to school, and there was no way out of it. Before that week, I don't think I had ever missed a day of school before—though I remember a conversation with Mom one time when I tried.

"Ma, I feel really bad. My stomach hurts. Can I stay home today?" I asked.

"Now, Dwight, you're well enough to talk to me," she said. "Where are you bleeding? Is your arm broken? If I don't have to take you to the hospital, you're well enough to go to school. You know the rules." School was serious business in our family.

That week was a blur of activity and emotions. I would sometimes come upon Mom crying in one room and then find Grandmother Venice crying in another. They moved as if in a daze. Finally, I went to my older brother and said, "Cedrick, Dad always told us to be strong no matter what. I think this is what he meant. We need to help out because nothing's getting done." Cedrick agreed, and for the next week, we prepared most of the meals and did all the chores around the house. We tended the garden and picked the vegetables. We did everything we could to keep things going. Mom and Grandmother Venice arranged the funeral, met with Reverend Evans, and just tried to survive from one moment to the next.

Dad's funeral was standing-room-only at New Hopewell Missionary Baptist Church. Flowers and pictures of him were placed throughout the church. Reverend Evans had been our pastor since before I was born, and he conducted a moving memorial. The casket was open, but all of us children refused to go up and look. We didn't want to remember our Dad in a coffin. Instead, we sat huddled together in the front pew. I was afraid to look at him, and I kept my head down during the entire eulogy, fearful that I might get a glimpse of Dad by accident.

Reverend Evans spoke of my Dad's high school infatuation with Lesa, my Mom. He spoke of Dad's love for us kids and how he wanted us to lead the best lives we could. He joked that it would take an earthquake or worse for Dad to let us miss school. He talked about how Dad was a true and loving friend, how he loved cars, and how he worked hard every day. And Reverend Evans also spoke of forgiveness and the importance of not taking the law into our own hands. He clearly felt the tension Dad's murder had sparked in the community and wanted to calm the waters around him.

Other people stood to speak as well, expressing their sorrow, sharing memories of Dad, and even telling some funny stories about his life. Because of the way Dad had died, there was a sense that this was more than a normal funeral. The whole community felt personally wounded, and so it was a community event. We all wanted a sense of closure for this tragedy, and everyone felt strength and comfort in sharing their feelings at the memorial service.

When the church service was over, the pallbearers took Dad to the hearse and loaded him inside. The cemetery was located on church property, so everybody just walked over to Dad's burial site. As I moved with the crowd, I was surprised at its size. It has only been with time that I've realized how deeply my father's murder affected our small community.

Reverend Evans finished with the "Ashes to ashes, dust to dust" prayer from the Book of Common Prayers, and we went home still grieving and confused. As we gathered at our house, family members hugged and cried, and we all did our best to celebrate and remember Dad's life. But not everybody was in a grieving mood, and I happened upon a remarkable conversation shortly after we got home.

"You know the police ain't never gonna find the bastard who did this. They'll sit on their fat asses and just let it fade away," one of my uncles said, not knowing I was listening off to the side.

Another of my uncles added, "Whoever did this wanted to send a message. He won't be able to keep his mouth shut. We'll find out who it is, and we'll give him a message of our own."

"We can't just let this stand," a third uncle chimed in, "We can't just ignore it like nuthin' ever happened. We gotta send our own message."

Grandmother Venice was standing nearby listening to her three sons, and I could see her face grow angrier by the second.

"Well, I am so proud to have raised you three fools," she burst in, "Will revenge make you happy? What will you gain by taking the law into your own hands? Nothing. All you'll do is make matters worse. You can't bring Dwight back, and I'll be visiting your foolish selves in jail until I die. Is that what you want? Will that help anybody?" she asked, staring them down. Grandmother Venice was the matriarch of the family, and you opposed her at your own risk.

"The way you get your revenge is to love people no matter what," she continued forcefully. "You don't solve one killing by doing another. I raised you better than that. If you take matters into your own hands, you bring this family down to the killer's level, and we're better than that. You're better than that. I want you to cherish Dwight's memory and keep him in your heart. That's true strength. Don't let me hear you talking about revenge or giving lessons to anybody ever again."

My grandmother had spoken, and that was the law of the family. My uncles were boiling with anger and wanted to do something about it, but they also knew Grandmother Venice was right. They let the matter go, and to my knowledge, nobody ever raised the topic again.

The funeral was over, but talk of the murder continued for the next month. Nobody ever came forward to identify the driver or confirm whether or not there were other passengers. The police had leads, but no charges were ever brought against potential suspects. We heard rumors of a man bragging about killing my Dad and teaching us all a lesson, but nothing was ever proved. In the months and years that followed, Dad's murder melted into the town's collective memory and became part of its history.

2

WE WERE POOR BUT DIDN'T KNOW IT

I stayed awake most nights during the week following my Dad's death, and more than once I cried myself to sleep. I know my brothers and sister did the same. Dad was no longer there to take us on rides in his Trans Am…He wasn't there smiling and teasing us for the silly things we did…And he wasn't there to answer our questions.

No question was off-limits to Dad. He might not answer us, but we were allowed to ask him anything on our minds, and he would never get angry.

"Dad, why did you and Mom get divorced?" I asked one day when he was alone with Cedrick and me. He didn't want to go there, but he also knew that this affected our lives.

"Guys, parents aren't perfect, and I'm living proof of that," Dad answered. "Your Mom and I were deeply in love when we got married. We still love each other—but now it's a different kind of love. You can love somebody and still not want to live with them," he explained. "And Mom and I didn't live together well.

"We knew it would be hard on you kids if we broke up," Dad went on. "But we thought it would hurt even worse if we lived together arguing all the time. We weren't happy in our lives together. There are few things we can really know in life, but I know this: I love you more than anything in the world. I only want the best for you, and I'll be there to do anything I can to ease your way. I'm not going anywhere, and I'll always be around to make sure you go to school every day."

After Dad's death, I could still recall every word of that conversation, and it rang in my ears as if Dad had somehow betrayed us. He said he would be there every day, and now he wasn't. I knew it wasn't his fault he'd been shot, but maybe if he were still living with us, this wouldn't have happened. I loved him, but I was angry. He was Dad. He was everything. Now he was gone.

None of us kids wanted to go back to school the following Monday, but life had to get back to some sense of normalcy. We got on the bus unsure of what the day would bring, and as we passed MacDonald's Store, we saw a large swath of dried blood on the side of the road where my father had died.

I saw it each day for the next two weeks until the rain finally washed the stain away. It seemed like the final remnants of my Dad were slowly fading into the universe until he disappeared completely.

The students and teachers greeted us with tenderness and sympathy when we got back. They had gathered donations and purchased cards and a gift basket for us, and one of my teachers dedicated the class period to me. She explained how sorry she and my classmates were for the loss I'd suffered and how happy they all were to have me back. She didn't shy away from the events of the past week, and she helped everybody face the tragedy head-on. The kids expressed their feelings in an open and honest way, and this helped us deal with our feelings and confront our fears. In retrospect, it was the best thing she could have done and the quickest path to healing the class.

Up to sixth grade, I had been a decent student and gotten good grades, but I never thought much about it one way or another. A few weeks after Dad's death, however, things changed. I had a vivid dream about him that continues to affect me to this day. Dad appeared with a big smile on his face—the same kind of smile he had always worn in life. We went fishing at the pond near our house, and I caught more fish than I had ever caught before. As I reeled them in, Dad told me, "Dwight, each fish is a blessing in your life. You have more blessings than you can imagine, and you have many important things to do in the years ahead. Everything is going to be fine, and I'll be with you every step of the way. I'll never break that promise."

I awoke in the middle of the night startled by my dream and by the fact that I wasn't down at the pond fishing with my father. It had seemed so real. Had Dad really come back to visit me? Where was he? What did it mean? I felt his presence, and I believed he wanted to send me a message.

Dad had always wanted us to do the best we could in our studies because he had dropped out of high school. He believed education was the best path to a good life. After the dream, I made a vow that I would do everything I could to excel in school. This was the one message Dad stressed constantly, and I would honor his memory by doing my best. I kept that promise: I was a straight-A student every year of high school and most semesters of college. I never failed to take school seriously.

Life went on, and later that year we got a new addition to the family, my cousin Greg, who was my age. Greg's dad had problems with drugs, and his mother couldn't stand the strain. She asked if our mother would raise him, which Mom agreed to at once. We loved Greg and knew he would be much better off with us. He was already like a brother to us, and he became part of the immediate family. We went to school together, played sandlot football together, and argued with him like he was one of us.

The community of Hot Coffee was poor, and people were mostly concerned with just getting by and having the basic necessities. Our family lived in a crowded trailer for most of my childhood, and it never kept the rain out. There was no heating or cooling, but we had a roof over our heads. It was a huge deal for us when we were finally able to purchase a small brick home later in my sixth grade year. It was the first time I ever slept in a bedroom, which I shared with Voncarie, and it felt like we had achieved a huge milestone.

To support us, Mom worked full time at a chicken factory called Sanderson Farms and put in extra hours whenever she could. She cooked for the family before going to work and again when she got home, and she never seemed to rest. We had a large garden and grew most of our own vegetables. All the kids helped plant, weed, pick, and clean the bounty. We had tomatoes, green beans, peas, onions, butter beans, and much more. Every meal in season included something from the garden—and sometimes that was the whole meal. There was also a large pond near our home, and several days a week Cedrick and I would go fishing and bring back a string of bream and catfish for dinner. We'd clean the fish, and Mom had a hundred different ways of preparing them. She was a great cook and could make the most modest offering seem like a feast. Meat was a rare treat. We didn't keep any guns in the house for hunting, but our uncles were hunters, and it was a time for celebration when they sometimes dropped by with venison during hunting season.

We were poor but didn't know it. We always had food to eat, a place to sleep, and a roof over our heads.

At school, however, our clothes gave us away. They represented status on the schoolyard. We would pass clothing down from one sibling to the next until shirts and trousers were too threadbare to wear. Grandmother Venice could work miracles with a needle and thread, and she made trousers, shirts, sweatshirts, and shoes last for years. Our clothes passed from Cedrick to me to Voncarie, so that by the time Voncarie got a pair of pants, it had more patches than an Eagle Scout uniform.

Our clothes became the target of much teasing at Collins Middle School, the school for kids from Hot Coffee and the surrounding towns. Nobody in the student body, which was about half black and half white, was wealthy, but we had less than most. We envied kids who wore shirts with actual labels or shoes without holes.

"Hey, Dwight," a kid named Jimmy said one day. "Why don't you buy a new shirt this year? That one's starting to stink."

"My shirt may not be fancy, but at least I know how to wash myself. You should try it once in a while," I answered. Exchanges like this sometimes led to a scuffle, but punishment at home always felt worse than any battle at school.

There were three big rules in our home. The first, as I've mentioned, was that we had to go to school no matter what. The second was that we all had to attend church every Sunday. Not only that, but we also had to be active in some church activity during the week. We were raised as Baptists, and Christian teachings were a part of our daily lives. The third rule was that fighting would not be tolerated. Not ever. Not for any reason. There was always a better answer.

"Dwight, you know better," Mom would say when I'd come home after a schoolyard fight. "You don't have to bring yourself down to the lowest level just because somebody else does. Did you accomplish anything?" I'd sometimes think to myself, "Yeah, I punched him in the head," but I never dared say it out loud.

"Words can only hurt you if you let them," my mother would go on. "You know better."

It felt like I went from one embarrassment at school to another embarrassment at home, and it wasn't fair. My good fortune, however, was that Cedrick had a shorter fuse than I did, and so he was more likely to get Mom's lecture. And to their great credit, the teachers at Collins were quick to put a stop to this kind of teasing. They understood that many of their students lived in poverty, and they would not tolerate making fun of people because of it. For the most part, everybody got along and accepted their circumstances. It was just the way things were.

In seventh grade, I found a new love: football. Cedrick was now playing football in high school, and I became a starter in middle school. Voncarie was still in elementary school, but anything Cedrick, Greg, and I did, he wanted to do as well. As things turned out, Cedrick and I were excellent players, but Voncarie was the natural athlete in the family. He became a local star, got a full scholarship to Ohio University, and developed into a professional talent. Today he plays football overseas.

Greg wanted to join the team as well, but he had a totally different body type. He was short and lean, and while he tried his best, football was not his sport. The four of us boys would work out together all the same, spot each other when we lifted weights, play sandlot football every chance we got, and generally learn life's lessons together. Football and other sports kept us out of trouble, and they kept Mom happy because she knew where we were all the time. We four boys became inseparable over the years, and we have remained best friends throughout our lives. Our Dad's death forced us all to grow up a little faster than we might have otherwise, and we came to depend on each other for support throughout our youth.

But we had our own unique way of showing that support. "Dwight, you're slower than grandma," Cedrick would scoff. "Plus you lift weights like a little girl. This is a man's sport." All four of us pushed ourselves and each other hard—which meant a lot of merciless teasing.

Collins Middle School was a football powerhouse, and we went undefeated for the two years I played there. I played linebacker and defensive line positions in middle school. Cedrick was becoming a star defensive lineman in high school, and he usually played nose tackle and some fullback. I couldn't wait to play high school ball too. I worked out every day to prepare—lifting weights, doing wind sprints, practicing at various positions. It was a fun—and legal—way to release energy. I loved the physical contact of football, and I would dream about tackling running backs.

My middle school years were filled with sports, friends, fishing, and family. It was a joyful period. But the four years of high school were the most fun of my life. My world grew larger, and I loved my life. I loved sports. I had a girlfriend. I excelled academically, and I was a "big man on campus." It was perfect.

I played football for all four years of high school, and I was the starting center on varsity beginning my sophomore year. Between my freshman and sophomore years, I grew another six inches in height and added sixty pounds to my weight. It was a growth spurt that was all muscle. I went from five feet eight to six feet two and from 160 to 220 pounds. I had beaten out a junior and a senior to win the starting center position, and I took the job seriously. I lifted weights constantly and became one of the strongest players on the team, even as a sophomore. Later that year, I also played defensive line and was one of only two sophomores to play both offense and defense. When football season ended, I was on the track-and-field team and excelled at shot put. It was a great feeling to press the shot put firmly against my neck, spin rapidly to gather the perfect momentum, and then hurl the shot put as far as I could. I practiced this for hours on end and was never bored for a moment.

I had a great relationship with my coaches, and I came to admire them for the time they spent with us and the work they did to make us good people as well as excellent players. In many ways, they were substitute father figures for me and my brothers. It was because of them that I knew early on that I wanted to play football as long as I could. When that was done, I wanted to coach.

Coach Bender sometimes put me in charge of the offensive line during practice, and I worked out at several positions—guard, tackle, and center. We would often have two-on-two drills, and two of the guys were white, and two were black. Coach would say, "Okay, guys. Time for the Oreo drills." We would joke about our salt and pepper workouts, and whenever it was black against white, there would be a lot of teasing.

"Pepper, stand by. We're gonna grind you into tiny pieces," the white guys would say.

"Salt, you get ready 'cause we're gonna turn you into dead meat, which is where you belong."

The football team was very close, and the trash talking was always in good fun. I never once saw any racial conflict in the school, and every member of the team was protective of the others. We grew closer still when tragedy hit the team.

I grew up with a kid named Eric Barnes. We attended elementary and middle school together, and he lived nearby. Eric would join us every day for pick-up football and basketball games, and he was like a member of the family. He was a year older than me, and he was a running back. We called him "Black Ninja" because he had dark skin and was super fast. At the start of my sophomore year, we were all looking forward to his being a big part of the team's success.

But one night after a football game that year, he went out drinking with some friends to celebrate. Drinking was new to Eric, and he didn't know how to handle alcohol or understand its effects. I wasn't there, but I heard all the stories. Eric drank far more than he could handle, and he wandered off from the group. Drunk and tired, he lay down to sleep in the middle of Highway 84. A passing truck didn't see him in time, and Eric was killed instantly. He was seventeen, a stunning young man with a vast future in front of him, who had his life cut short because of one indiscretion. The school community was shocked and horrified, and the football team was distraught. We somehow kept our spirits together, however, and we dedicated the season to him. The players stenciled his jersey number onto our cleats, and the team bonded even more closely than before. From that moment on, we all looked after each other and did our best to protect each other every way we could. Eric's tragic death was not my first brush with alcohol, and so I vowed that I would not let it destroy my life as it had his. I made the decision never to drink, and since that day, I haven't taken a single sip of alcohol. For that, I thank my dear friend Eric.

By the time I was in my junior year, the team had improved dramatically, and we received a state ranking for the first time in many years. This was a big step up for the school, and we put heart and soul into being the best team we could be. We made the playoffs all three years I played varsity, but our hearts were broken during my sophomore season, the year Eric died. The opposing school scored a touchdown in the final seconds of the game and then completed a two-point conversion, which provided the margin of victory. We lost in the playoffs the following year to our school rival, which was another bitter pill to swallow.

I continued to work hard and was a standout on the team. We had many good players, however, and college football scouts would often come by practice to look for prospects. I expected to win a full football scholarship to the University of Southern Mississippi, but fate had different plans.

During one game early in my senior year, I wrenched my knee and didn't tell anybody. I was limping and in pain, but I didn't want to come out of the game. If I could stand, I could play. That was the motto in our family, and it was a simple but misguided formula. I managed the best I could, made it through the game, and assumed it was just a minor sprain that would heal in a few days. Instead, the pain persisted for weeks, but I kept on playing and managed to perform without any signs of a limp. But the coach still noticed a drop-off in my play and started asking questions.

"Dwight, you're not playing up to your talent. What's up? Is something wrong?" he asked. I assured him I was fine and could do the job. He believed me.

After the season was over and I was still in pain, I realized I had to see a doctor. The diagnosis was harsh. I had torn a muscle and some cartilage in my knee, and it would take at least a year to repair. Even after that year, my knee would probably buckle and cause me trouble in the future. My playing days were over, and my dreams of stardom as a Golden Eagle at USM evaporated. It was a big blow, but I still harbored hopes of getting better and making my way onto the team as a walk-on as a sophomore in college. I ended up getting an academic scholarship to USM, but I never played football again.

During all that time as a high school athlete, I had been giving just as much time to my schoolwork. As I had promised Dad I would, I took my studies seriously. I loved math, and my teachers were excellent. They made it fun, and math came easily to me. Each new challenge was like doing a crossword puzzle. I would often try to solve math problems while in other classes. I started to develop an interest in computers as well, and I enjoyed working on technical problems of any kind. I didn't know it then, but this would become a big part of my life as the years passed.

I was on the honor roll each year, participated in many after-school activities, joined the Math Club, and was a member of the Beta Club—a club for top students that was alien territory for most football players. We got to participate in many special events with other schools, travel to various academic competitions across the state, and even visit some college campuses. My football coach started calling me "Mr. Beta," and I was recognized in the school for both my academic and athletic accomplishments.

A couple of months before high school graduation, I received an unexpected honor. The faculty selected four graduating seniors that year for the "Collins High School Hall of Fame," and I was one of them. This was based on academic achievement, school spirit, athletic prowess, and overall contributions to the school during the past four years. The school takes a picture of each person selected and places it in the main hallway along with a brief history of each student's accomplishments. My picture hangs there to this day, and whenever Cedrick or Voncarie get a little too full of themselves for their athletic success in high school, I simply ask: "Guys, whose picture is still hanging in the main hallway?"

When graduation finally came, I felt like I had become a man. I had earned an academic scholarship. I was ready for college. And mostly, I was eager for the future to reveal itself to me.

3

CHASING A DREAM

Life in high school was fun and engaging during my senior year, but we had some problems at home. Mom had gotten remarried, and my stepfather was verbally abusive and physically threatening to her and my siblings. I was a big, strong guy who towered over him, and he kept his temper in check whenever I was around. He knew I would protect my family, and he didn't want to confront me directly.

"Mom, I'm gonna wait a semester before I go to USM," I told her. "I promise I'll go to college and graduate, but I'm not leaving while he's here. That's all there is to it."

I think Mom was secretly happy with my decision, but she put up a big fuss all the same. "Dwight, you say you'll go to college, but life can get in the way," she argued. "We can handle things here. I want you to go to school and make us proud."

I was eager to get started at USM, but I was more fearful that my family would be at risk if I left. Cedrick had joined the Navy immediately after high school, and he was overseas. Voncarie was several years younger than me, and I didn't want him to have to take on this role. Greg had moved out a couple of years before to live with his grandmother. That left only me. I was now the man of the family.

"Mom, I'll start next semester if everything's okay at home. That's all there is to it," I said again. I decided to defer college for one semester so I could help around the house, earn some money for the family, and make sure nothing bad happened to Mom or my siblings.

My stepfather left during this period, and it was a moment of celebration for the family. I felt like a big burden had been taken off my shoulders. I was free to start college; my siblings were rid of my stepfather's temper; and Mom was free to pursue her own happiness. It was time to begin a new phase in my life.

I started at the University of Southern Mississippi in January 2001, and I arranged to share a dorm room with my life-long friend, Lee Barnes. We walked the campus for a few hours the day I arrived, and I was thrilled by what I saw—students moving from class to class, imposing buildings, state-of-the-art athletic facilities, and a sense of purpose all around me. And…there were also attractive women at every turn. I was something of a class clown in high school, and I was also a flirt. I fancied myself a ladies' man, and I was in heaven. USM was the one school I had wanted to attend above all others for years, and it was the only college I applied to. It was everything I had hoped for and more.

I grew up with Lee, and we have been close friends all our lives. He was one of many students from Collins High School who attended USM, and I knew many other people on campus as well. Sharing a room with Lee, however, proved to be a mixed blessing. We were both serious students, but we were also pranksters and very competitive with each other. If he played a joke on me, I had to do one better on him. If I did well on a test, he wanted to do better. We pushed each other to do our best, but we also made life harder than it needed to be.

"Damn, Lee. What's wrong with this iron? It's spraying out black junk," I complained one day.

Lee could barely contain his laughter but suggested it was probably just a little rust. I finally saw the half-empty bottle of Coke sitting on the TV and realized what he had done. He'd filled the iron with Coke instead of water hoping he would be around the next time I used it.

"You're an idiot, Lee. I don't mind a joke, but you just ruined my shirt."

Lee was unrepentant. "Well, dopey, you may recall hiding my textbooks before our last science exam," he said. "This hardly makes up for forcing me to pull an all-nighter."

I was far from innocent and couldn't protest much. "Well, we're even then," I said, but Lee didn't feel the scales of justice were quite balanced yet.

A few days later, just before I took my seat in the dining hall, he poured some bleach on my chair. My behind started to itch, but I didn't pay it much attention until I stood up after the meal and the other students started laughing. My trousers were stained white; my butt was itching; and I looked ridiculous. Lee and I were close friends, but that friendship was tested more than once during my first semester. After the semester was over, he and I decided that if we wanted to survive through our sophomore year, we would probably be better off with different roommates.

I dated several girls that first semester and made many new friends, but I knew my priorities. I got straight A's and made the President's List. I never missed an opportunity to have fun or go out with my friends, but I also never strayed from my real purpose of getting a first class education. I knew I wanted to graduate with my class, so I took at least one extra course each semester to make up for my late start. I also took at least one course each summer to build up extra credits and clear my schedule for senior year.

By the time I was a sophomore, I had a good idea of what I wanted to do when I graduated. I loved math and computers, and I loved sports, especially football. The football coaches I had in middle and high school were my heroes. They had helped me in ways I didn't understand at the time, and they were a consistent and steadying influence on my life. I wanted to be involved with sports and coach football—preferably on the high school level. I decided to become a teacher. I wanted to be the same type of example for children that those coaches had been for me, and I took a broad range of courses that would prepare me for multiple teaching certifications.

I am a social person, and I enjoyed spending time with people in my Business and Technology major. We would work on computers together, play lots of video games, and go to sporting events. I also joined the Fraternity of Masons. Lee had joined before me, and he would often spend weekends volunteering in projects to help the community. He worked at homeless shelters and at outings for kids, and he was making a real contribution to people around him. I admired what he was doing, and I began to study the history of the Masons. I liked what I learned and decided I wanted to be a part of it as well. I became a Mason in my junior year and was active in various student projects over the next two years.

My one indiscretion during this time was getting a tattoo. I got a Golden Eagle, the symbol for USM, on my left arm. I wanted to show my association with the school. I don't like the idea of young people getting tattoos, but I still look at my Golden Eagle periodically and fondly recall my college days at USM.

By the time I was a senior, I had completed almost all the course work needed to graduate, including many courses in math, computer science, marketing and finance, physical and special education, and technology. I was an honor student and received only one C during the previous three years. It was in geology, and much of the course work involved identifying different types of rocks by sight. Try as I might, I struggled. I couldn't tell shale from sandstone or gold from pyrite. We went rock hunting several times during the course, which was the kind of activity I enjoyed more than classroom lectures, but that didn't help. I felt like I had rocks in my head, but I managed to pass. I kept wishing I had taken astronomy or chemistry instead.

At the beginning of my senior year, I started student teaching. I spent a few weeks at several schools observing different classes and then began teaching myself. I loved it. The schools varied dramatically in their culture and the composition of their student bodies. I taught at Mendenhall High School, which was predominantly white and middle class, and I also taught at Taylorsville High, which was just a few miles from my rural home and largely black. They were worlds apart in many ways, but the material was still the same. I started to refine my thinking about what kind of teacher I wanted to be, and I paid close attention to different teaching styles. Each teacher approached their students quite differently from class to class. Their example helped me to understand that I wanted to be true to my personality while still helping students get full value for the time and effort they invested in my class.

One of the teachers I observed at length was Mrs. Marsha Magee at Mendenhall High School. The students and I all loved her. She was full of energy and positive spirit. She constantly asked the kids questions, joked with them, and brought out the best in them. She would praise them publicly for their good work, but she also wasn't afraid to gently chide them to do better when they came up short. She never had any disciplinary problems in her classes because the kids were too busy having fun, learning new things, and working on projects to get into any trouble. Her affection for the students was genuine, and they didn't want to disappoint her. She was magic. She was the teacher I wanted to become.

"Dwight, teaching is about the kids, not about the teacher," she advised me. "You can bore them to death, and they'll still probably learn something. But they won't learn passion or take new perspectives to heart. Many of the things we are teaching are new to them. The kids need time to digest and internalize what we've covered, so I like to give them that chance. Fill the class with stories or anecdotes. Tell a joke once in a while. It relieves the pressure and makes learning less stressful for everybody."

Mrs. Magee was a delight as a teacher and an even better mentor. She took her work seriously, but that didn't mean she couldn't have fun with it. I learned from her that fun is often the best path to knowledge, and I wanted to make it a big part of my classroom.

Early in my final semester at USM, I attended a job fair on campus for prospective teachers. The first table I came to was sponsored by Laurel High School, which is about thirty miles from where I lived. I gave a copy of my resume and transcript to Carolyn Stone, the principal of Laurel High, and we chatted for a long while. At the end of our conversation, Ms. Stone said: "Dwight, you are just what I'm looking for, and I'd love for you to teach at Laurel High." She invited me to visit the school, which was music to my ears, and she asked me to observe several classes before I started student teaching that semester.

"Dwight, our teacher for Discovery Technology is retiring next year, and you would be a perfect replacement for him. I'd like you to sit in on a few of his classes and see what you think. What do you say?" she asked. My heart jumped, and I couldn't believe the opportunity that was before me. I agreed immediately because this was the course I most wanted to teach: technology and math. I visited the school on several occasions and liked what I saw. It would be a great fit for me: I liked the students, the faculty, and especially the course material. Then I got a special opportunity.

I had received my teaching certification already, and my mentor teachers had given me great recommendations. My course work at USM was complete, and I was already substitute teaching during my senior year. Then, not long after I first met Ms. Stone, her Discovery Technology teacher at Laurel High School became ill and had to retire two months before the school year ended. Ms. Stone asked me to finish the year for him. I jumped at the chance to get two months of hands-on experience under my belt before starting full-time teaching in the fall. It was an exciting learning opportunity, and I connected well with the kids. I was pumped. It wasn't easy to take over a class that was already deep into the year, but the kids accepted the situation, and I got a broader perspective on the course that would hold me in good stead for the upcoming year.

My graduation from USM was a big day for my family. I was the first one in my family to attend and graduate from college, and everybody was proud of my accomplishment. Pastor Evans asked me to speak before the congregation, tell them about college, and stand as an example for the kids coming behind me. Then he stood to speak, and there were tears in the eyes of many parishioners. We all knew each other, and my graduation was a point of pride for the community. Pastor Evans mentioned how proud my dad would have been, and I had to fight back the tears. Dad had never been far from my thoughts, and my graduation marked the fulfillment of the promise I had made to him long ago. At the end of the service, the pastor gave me a Bible with my name engraved on it. I treasure it to this day.

My graduation party was at a local seafood buffet. My family, friends, and church group took over the place for the evening. One of their own had made good, and everybody celebrated and savored the moment.

I received several job offers from other schools but accepted the position at Laurel High. I was an attractive candidate to many schools because of my good grades and range of courses in college, but I am also a black man. Many schools needed and wanted more men on the faculty, and being black was a bonus. Laurel High was mostly black, and this gave me some instant credibility. When I accepted the position at Laurel, I already knew many of the students, liked and respected the faculty, and thoroughly enjoyed the material I was going to teach. My only regret was that there was no opening for a coach on the football team. That dream would have to wait.

My first full year of teaching was a wake-up call every day. Teachers often say they learn more from their students than the students learn from them, and I know that to be true. I was all of twenty-one years old my first year of teaching, and some of the students in my homeroom classes were eighteen or nineteen. Since I was not far removed in age from many of them, I was challenged once or twice because of it along the way.

"Dwight, why you wastin' our time on this?" one of my older students asked.

I replied calmly but in a no-nonsense tone. "Akeem, the first thing to remember is my name is Mr. Owens. I've earned that respect and insist upon it. 'Dwight' may be my first name, but I'm the teacher and you're the student. Call me Mr. Owens." That may sound harsh, but if you get too familiar with the students you tend to lose their respect. I wasn't going to let that happen. "Secondly, Akeem, the Discovery Technology course is about things you are going to encounter throughout your life. We do a lot of work with computers, robotics, film, videography, recording, and computer software. All these things will be a part of your life at some point, and many students will end up making a living in these fields. It can only help to have some exposure with them. Since you're here anyway, you might as well learn everything you can. It won't hurt." I was six feet two and 220 pounds of muscle, and I loomed over most of the students. I think my physical presence alone tended to put a damper on this kind of challenge from students.

Mostly, the kids were enthusiastic and bright eyed. Classes were forty-five minutes long, and I always gave the kids three minutes at the start of the class to talk among themselves. This let them get caught up on the day's events, share personal information, and ease more comfortably into the work we were doing that day. I took many pages from Ms. Magee's book, and I interacted with the kids in a fun way. I never raised my voice; I sought and considered their suggestions for class projects, and I always had a joke or story at the ready, often about some mistake I had made along the way. I also asked the kids to keep a journal in the class and submit it to me each week. The journal was intended to let them express their views openly and honestly, talk about areas they were struggling with, and give me a better read on the class. I never shared the journals with anybody else or talked about anything personal the kids said in them, and they came to trust me completely.

The journals took on a life of their own, and I learned things about the kids that were astonishing. One student had no mother and had to wake up her younger siblings each morning, cook breakfast, and get them ready for school. She then cooked dinner and basically managed the house while her dad was at work. Another wrote that she already had two children of her own at home and was trying desperately to make it through high school and be a good example for them. Some of the stories were heartbreaking and others were laugh-out-loud funny.

"Mr. Owens, I didn't do my homework on Tuesday because I was sitting on a tree limb fishing and it broke and I fell in the mud. My mom was fire mad and made me do the laundry for the whole family that night. I lost my fishing pole and didn't even catch any fish." Such is life in a rural town.

In many ways I was a role model for the kids, but there was a danger in that. One of the principals I had spoken with along the way gave me a serious lecture on the particular dangers of spending time alone with any female students, so I always made sure there was somebody else in the room. I was not willing to take the risk of being seen alone with a female student, and there were good reasons for my caution. Kids sometimes get a crush on their teachers, and given my youth, I was a prime candidate for this. I would have none of it, however, and I let my actions speak for themselves. I was always accessible to any student who needed help, but I was not going to risk my career or reputation in the process.

I loved the kids, and I loved teaching, but some of their situations broke my heart. Laurel High was a great school, but like all schools, kids brought their upbringing and family life into the classroom. On one occasion, two girls got into a fight on school grounds. We stopped it immediately and called their parents in for a conference. This usually has the effect of calming things down, and it gives the kids something to think about before meeting with their parents and members of the school administration.

This time, things were different. When the mother of one of the young girls arrived for the conference, she asked her daughter, "Is this the girl you fought with?"

When her daughter said she was, the mom looked at the other girl and said, "You just better watch out. My girl's gonna beat your ass later on."

I was shocked at this response. Both girls were suspended for a couple of days, and we made sure they were separated when they got back. The lesson was clear, however. This girl had learned some hard lessons from her mom, who clearly thought fighting was the best way to resolve problems. I knew that young lady had a tough road ahead of her.

I enjoyed every minute of my year at Laurel High, but I also wanted to coach football. One of my high school football coaches, Coach Jackson, had become the principal of Collins Middle School but he was still an assistant coach at Collins High. I learned that he was interviewing people at a job fair and looking for prospective teachers, so I went to speak with him.

It was like old times. Coach Jackson told me, "If you come to Collins, we'll always have a coaching position available for you. You were already helping us coach when you were on the team in high school, and you'd be great at it." Coach Jackson said he had a teaching position for Special Education and Math at Collins Middle School, and he just needed to get approval from the school board to finalize an offer. He got his approvals, made a formal offer within the week, and I accepted on the spot. Not only was I going to teach at my alma mater, I was going to be an assistant coach for my old high school team and one of my personal heroes. I loved Laurel High, but this was simply an offer I couldn't refuse.

I spoke with Ms. Stone, and while she was sorry to see me go, she understood and supported me in my decision. I explained how much I loved teaching and was grateful for the opportunity she'd given me to teach at Laurel High.

"Ms. Stone," I told her, "I gained confidence and developed my teaching skills under your guidance. I will always appreciate the way you reached out to me. Thank you."

But I had never hidden my desire to be a football coach, so Ms. Stone simply said, "Dwight, you have a wonderful career ahead. Collins is lucky to have you, and I wish you every success."

I finished the year on a high note, and I looked forward to teaching and coaching in the year ahead. It was a dream come true.

4

LIFE TURNED UPSIDE DOWN

"Voncarie, I'll meet you and Cedrick at Ram Motors 'round four o'clock," I told my younger brother. "The district rally should be over early this afternoon, and that'll give me time to get there."

"Sounds good to me. Just make sure your sorry self shows up on time," he joked and hung up.

I took a deep breath because I knew this was going to be a packed day. A good day.

It was Friday morning, August 5, 2005, and the family was excited because my younger brother, Voncarie, had won a full football scholarship to Ohio University. He was going to be a Bobcat, the perfect name for him since he was sleek, strong, and had an attitude on the football field. He was a terrific athlete with a good sense of humor, and he would always laugh whenever I said, "Voncarie, you're just lucky I was around to teach you everything you know."

My brother Cedrick and I were going to meet Voncarie after work and help him buy a car so he could get back and forth from college. I had a friend who worked at the dealership, and he had helped me buy my first vehicle. He already had a deal set up for us. Cedrick and I had both saved a few dollars and wanted to contribute what we could to make sure Voncarie got a fitting going-away gift. He'd earned it, and we were proud of our baby brother. And maybe I was just a bit jealous because I never got to play in college. I knew he loved football and would enjoy every minute of his time at Ohio.

It was about eight in the morning, and after the call, I left for school. It was drizzling, and football practice had been cancelled that day because of the district rally for the teachers. We couldn't do both things at once, and this proved more fortunate than I could have ever imagined. Most days I drove Maurice, one of the high school football players, home after practice. Not today. The district was preparing for the first day of school the following Monday, and I had to get my classroom ready for the special education and math courses I would be teaching that year. I wanted everything just right. After all, you only get one chance to make a first impression and set the tone for the year. I needed to be ready. Then I had to attend the rally, which started around 10 a.m., meet Cedrick and Voncarie at 4 p.m. to buy the car, and finally catch up with Tamika, a first-year teacher at nearby Laurel High School. We were preparing together for our supplemental teacher certification tests the next day, hers in math, mine in physical education. A lot to do, but all good things. It was a good time to be alive.

"Yo, Dwight. Are you pumped?" asked Coach Jackson.

"Sure am, Coach. I've been getting ready for this all summer. Can't wait for school to start," I answered. And then I smiled, realizing that although I had liked high school well enough growing up, I never thought I'd utter those words.

The rally lasted a few hours. We had motivational speakers, who talked about the challenges we faced in the coming year, and we discussed various legal issues and educational goals. The best part was getting to meet with friends and teachers from other schools in the district. We were all on the same team trying to do the best we could for our kids, and we all felt a sense of excitement and optimism as the new school year approached. We felt good, and we all enjoyed the fellowship and common goals we shared.

"See you Monday, Dwight. Don't let your 'puters catch no virus," Coach Jackson said in good humor as we left for the day.

"Not to worry, Coach," I answered with a smile.

It had been raining throughout the day and was still raining when I left the school. I'm a bit of a daredevil, but I respect the speed limit whenever the weather doesn't cooperate.

"Just about one thirty—plenty of time," I thought as I headed home to get my money. "It's a good thing I don't have Maurice with me today. Football practice would have been a mess."

It would only take about twenty minutes to get home, and I had enough time to get ready to meet my brothers in Hattiesburg. I was going over the day's events and thinking about school when I glanced in the rearview mirror.

"Damn. That guy is driving way too fast," I thought, seeing a big Chevy truck closing ground behind me. I assumed he'd just pass me and turned my eyes back to the road ahead.

Suddenly, with a loud clap of breaking glass and crunching metal, the Chevy slammed into the back of my car, and both of us immediately went into a tailspin. I swerved into the steep gully off Highway 84 and careened into a tree; the Chevy spun into a ditch on the other side of the road. I immediately passed out. For an instant, my mind flicked back into consciousness, and I whispered a prayer.

"Please save me, God."

A lot of things happened next, but I wasn't aware of any of them. Layne McClaurin, a close friend and fellow high school football player, was an EMT, and he was the first to appear on the scene. He told me later he got a cold chill and almost vomited when he realized it was me in the car. My torso was on the floor bent in an unholy way, and my legs were wrapped around the steering wheel. Blood everywhere, and no signs of life. I had my seatbelt on, but the impact was so violent that I got twisted and spun upside down into an unnatural position. Months later, Layne told me that he was so shaken by seeing me like that that he quit his job as an EMT. He just couldn't take the thought of going through that again.

All the normal things happened. The state police appeared, controlled traffic, and secured the scene of the accident. Members of the volunteer fire department were right behind them, and the ambulance crew had already started to work. My car was crushed, almost unrecognizable, and they had to use the Jaws of Life to get me out.

The other driver had just enough presence of mind to try to make a getaway. He was stuck in a ditch and doing everything he could to get his car out and flee the scene. He didn't succeed. I would later learn that his name was Herman Posey and he lived in a trailer about a mile down the road. He was seventy-one years old and something of a hermit. He lived alone, and his only known hobby was alcohol. He was a drunk, and he had been cited on four prior occasions for Driving Under the Influence. This time, he had done his worst. He was drunk again, and while he was cognizant enough to want to escape, he wasn't aware enough to know he had been speeding recklessly and had just crashed into the car in front of him. This time, his drunk driving had consequences that would last a lifetime—mine.

The ambulance sped to Collins Hospital, about five miles away. It was a small hospital with limited facilities, but it was the closest. The EMTs worked to get a heartbeat and stop my bleeding. All they could do was try to keep me alive long enough to get to the emergency room. Layne never took his eyes off me.

We got to the hospital, and everybody worked furiously. To no avail, it seemed. I barely had a pulse and no other signs of life. They stabilized me as best they could, put me on a ventilator, and prepared to take me to the larger Forrest General Hospital in Hattiesburg about twenty miles away. I was unconscious throughout these proceedings and during the trip to Forrest General. I was a whisper away from death. Maybe I was dead. I certainly wasn't in this world.

I was in a large field of bright flowers and luminous light. I sat there alone and watched as one scene after another from my childhood passed before me. I was riding on my three-wheel tricycle, a huge grin on my face, and I heard my Mom telling me to slow down. I saw my brothers and sisters…my parents and grandparents…my aunts and uncles. All the people who loved me. All the people who mattered so much to me. I saw myself making a tackle on the football field and then as a student teacher smiling at the kids. The dream went on and on. It seemed to last forever, and it was more real and more joyous than anything I had ever known before.

My dad, who died when I was in sixth grade, and my deceased aunts came to me, and I felt surrounded by a profound sense of peace and calm. They were enveloped by light, and my Dad looked at me with a gentle expression. He spoke softly.

"Dwight, it will be okay. It will be okay."

I was confused, but felt their intense love. They were emanating tranquility and a kind of love I had never felt before. They walked through a bright tunnel and disappeared into an intense ball of light. I started to follow…

"We've got him back!" yelled the attending physician. "I've got a pulse."

5

A HOSPITAL IS NOT A HOME

I opened my eyes to see wires, tubes, and medical equipment draped all over me. There were tubes in my mouth, my nose, and both sides of my ribcage. My vision was blurred, and I was confused, but I saw a flurry of people working on what seemed like every part of my body. I had no memory of the accident, and I wondered what the fuss was all about. I didn't understand what was going on. All I felt was the warm afterglow of my wonderful dream. Was I in heaven? Was this God's way of making death easy? I didn't understand any of it, but I was now conscious for good.

And my life was changed forever.

I had only spent a couple of hours at Collins Hospital where the doctors had performed an emergency operation to insert tubing under both sides of my rib cage to drain blood and fluid from around my lungs. At that time, nobody would be able to tell the extent of my injuries for several more days, but they did know my lungs needed immediate attention. Everybody realized that the situation was dire, and they had to act fast. They inserted breathing tubes, did the operation to drain my lungs, straightened my back, completed some preliminary tests, and stabilized me as best they could to prepare me for the trip to Forrest General Hospital in Hattiesburg. It was a much larger facility, and it was better equipped to deal with my injuries. The ambulance crew had known I would not survive the twenty-mile drive from the accident to Forrest General and decided to take me to Collins first. That was a good decision.

I didn't know it, but my mother and many family members arrived at Collins shortly after I did, and they filled up the emergency room. My mother had learned of the accident, dressed frantically, putting her shoes on the wrong feet, and driven straight to the site of the accident. When she saw my car, she said, "Please, Lord, let me see him one last time." She felt sure I could not have gotten out of that car alive.

My family and friends were frantic in the emergency room, and things only got worse when the doctors had to tell my mother that they were doing everything they could but she should prepare for the worst. They didn't think I would live through the night, but if I did, the next twenty-four hours would be the most critical. All my family could do at that point was pray, and that's just what they did. They locked arms and sent their plea out through space and time, asking God to let me live.

The Collins Hospital staff quickly arranged to transport me to Forrest General. Mom, of course, tried to join them in the ambulance, but couldn't because they had to work on me during transit. They needed extra EMTs onboard, and there was no space for her.

Layne was with me on the trip to Hattiesburg, although I didn't know it. I was still somewhere else, lost in a dream. He was there in the emergency room at Forrest General, and he was there when the doctor was finally ready to call my death. Layne said the doctor told him I'd been gone too long—there was no pulse, and it was over. But not for Layne it wasn't. He rejected the call and begged the doctor to keep searching for a pulse. He kept working on me himself and insisted the doctors do the same. Layne wasn't going to let his friend die without a fight. And it was then, miraculously and against all odds, that they found a pulse. I was still hanging on, and Layne was exuberant. His friend might make it yet.

When I opened my eyes some time later, and the doctor knew I was partly conscious, he softly said, "We almost lost you. Welcome back." I fell back asleep instantly and when I awoke, I was in the ICU. There was a crowd of people there, and I saw many friends and family members crying inside and outside the room. Mom was at my side.

My mother had formed a convoy and followed the ambulance to Forrest General. The medical staff tried to keep her out of the emergency room and ICU while they were working on me, but she would have none of it. They were doing their job as medical professionals, and Mom was doing hers as a mother. Mom won.

"I will not leave my son, and you're gonna need an army of security people to get me out of here," she said in a loud, no-nonsense voice. "And if you bring 'em, you'll have a heap of unconscious security guards to deal with as well."

They knew she wasn't going anywhere, and she didn't leave my side for a second. At one point, although I didn't know it, I opened my eyes to see her standing there, and I simply said, "Mom?" I then fell immediately back to sleep, and she thought I had died. The doctors assured her I was still alive, however, and she kept on watching and praying. Mom spent most of the next ten days at my bedside in the ICU and the two weeks after that with me when I was moved to my hospital room. The staff came to learn that that was just the way it was going to be, and they came to admire her persistence. But mostly they were afraid of her.

Word had gotten out quickly about the accident, and the emergency room at Forrest General was filled beyond capacity. There were over sixty of my relatives and friends there, and it was so crowded that the hospital had to start turning people away. They didn't want to do this to any of my friends, but they had no choice.

I spent the next ten days in excruciating, unrelenting pain in the ICU. The pain was constant, maddening. And in spite of all the life threatening injuries, my shoulder hurt worst of all. Burning and stabbing pain that wouldn't quit. Minute after minute, hour after hour. It consumed my thoughts, which might have been a good thing. I wasn't ready yet to deal with the bigger picture. And the doctors couldn't concern themselves with my shoulder at that point because it was not an immediate threat to my life. Nor could they give me the pain relief medicine they normally would have given, fearful of its reaction with other medication I was taking. My shoulder wasn't going to kill me. They had bigger problems to deal with.

It seemed like each time the doctors made progress in one area, a new problem would arise. We didn't know all the injuries at the time, and I'm not sure we ever will. I think that some of my injuries simply healed on their own over time. I do know that I will forever feel profound gratitude for the work this wonderful group of people did to keep me alive. Among other things, they had to contend with six broken ribs, punctured and severely battered lungs, a bruised kidney, hematoma, blood clots, extensive internal bleeding, a severed spinal cord, a broken back, inability to breathe on my own, a high and erratic fever, and a dislocated liver that had lodged in my chest cavity. The doctors and hospital staff had to deal with one emergency after another as I lay at death's door. I wasn't out of the woods for several weeks.

I was on a ventilator for my first three days at Forrest General. The extensive bruising in my lungs would heal over time, but the punctures were a different matter entirely. A severely punctured lung collapses. This is often life threatening and in my case was compounded by the collection of fluid in the vicinity. Although a damaged lung can often repair itself over time, the doctors at Collins had needed to insert tubes to drain the area and help me breathe. This was the first order of business, and while the operation saved my life, my breathing was labored and painful for the next three months.

I had to undergo breathing therapy every day after I got off the ventilator, and it was grueling. I had to force myself to breathe harder and harder with every breath despite all the pain until my breathing reached normal capacity. This was even more difficult because of my broken ribs, which protested angrily and caused a stabbing pain every time my lungs expanded even a little bit. If I didn't do this therapy, however, I would be susceptible to pneumonia and other infections that would most likely kill me in my weakened state. The therapy had to go on no matter what pain I was in.

There were other threats to my life as well, and my dislodged liver was perhaps the most dangerous. We only have one liver, and if we lose it, there is no chance of survival. After a major trauma like mine, organs can move around in the body. My liver had gone on its own odyssey and found a new home in my chest cavity. The doctors had to relieve the pressure from being lodged in an unnatural location and put my liver back where it belonged. This was no easy matter when I also had six broken ribs and punctured lungs in the neighborhood. I understand little about all this other than its being the first of many surgeries to come, and it was a big leap forward. It let me live one more day and fight the next battle.

Dr. Wiebe was the neurosurgeon treating me. He came into the ICU six days after I had arrived in Forrest General to do what I thought would be another set of tests. For the first several days, I had been trying to move my legs but couldn't. Dr. Donald, the trauma surgeon handling my case, had been treating me for the past week and had examined the results of every medical test imaginable. On this day, Dr. Wiebe checked my plantar fasciitis reflex by drawing a line with his fingers across the bottom of my feet. He wanted to see if my toes would wiggle or if he could get any response at all. He couldn't. I didn't feel a thing. As he pushed and prodded up my legs, I still felt nothing.

When he was finally done, he simply said, "Dwight, I'm sorry. You're paralyzed from the waist down."

Those words ring clearer today than they did when I first heard them. I wasn't ready to understand or cope with their meaning. I was more concerned about the pain I was suffering at that moment than what my life would become in the future. It would take weeks to understand the impact of Dr. Wiebe's statement.

Each day seemed to bring a new adventure in the ICU, and one day I woke up to find somebody sobbing in my room. It was an unexpected visitor, and I wasn't sure how to react. Nash Evans, a student at Laurel High, was there looking at me with tears streaming down his face. I had been his teacher in the technology course I taught at Laurel, and Nash was one of my most memorable students. He was a class clown and cut-up who didn't take school seriously enough. But he was smart, talented, and loved the spotlight. He enjoyed making presentations to the class and working with computers, robotics, and all kinds of technical devices. Nash also knew my first name was Dwight, and because I'm black, he would often joke, "Hey, de white guy is here." It was all in the spirit of good fun, and the class loved it.

But this day, Nash was no clown. He couldn't control his tears, and he was distraught. He had always been macho and tough; today he was overwhelmed with emotions and unable to deal with the sight of his once powerful teacher, now disabled.

Of course I tried to say the right things. "Hey, Nash, thanks for coming. That takes courage, and you should be proud. Tears are a good thing, you know. You can't live a good life without caring for other people." We talked a bit, but it was awkward and hard on both of us. I knew my teaching days were probably over, and it hurt because I also knew I could have helped many students who were just coming into their own—students who were beginning to open their eyes to new experiences and knowledge that would offer them better lives. Nash confessed that I was his favorite teacher, and I joked that he probably said that to all his teachers to get on their good side. Mostly we kept quiet, each in our own thoughts. Nash left that day with a host of feelings to sort through, and I was left with a memory that brings me joy whenever I turn back to it. It also made me think of another student who was now attending Collins High School.

Maurice Owens and I shared the same last name, but we weren't related. He was in my class when I was student teaching at Collins, and he was still there when I started coaching. Maurice was a great high school athlete and football player, and he always referred to me with the most respectful term he knew. He called me "Coach."

I would talk with Maurice about football, about college, about life at home. As with so many kids from broken homes raised in extremely difficult circumstances, Maurice was rebellious. He was a good kid, but he was struggling with his classes, with his responsibilities, and with how to become a man. There was a lot going on, and I had been through it all before him. I understood where he was coming from, and I hoped to nudge him in the right direction.

Maurice was smart, but he was also a smart aleck. He had plenty of brainpower, but he didn't know how to direct it. Getting a laugh in class was far more important to him than getting a good grade. I would drive Maurice home after football practice every day, and we talked constantly.

He said all the right things. "Hey, Coach, I'm serious about school and getting a football scholarship. I won't skip classes anymore, and I'll work more on my football skills."

I talked about my decision to become a teacher and about how disciplined thinking was far more important than getting a laugh in a classroom. I know Maurice appreciated the hand of friendship and the mentoring I provided, but he had a long road to travel.

I would have driven Maurice home on the day of my accident, but practice had been cancelled because of the teachers' rally. I even remember thinking it was a good thing he wasn't with me because it was raining so hard and the roads were treacherous. As time has passed, I have often wondered if this was God's hand at work. There were countless times this accident could have happened when I had Maurice with me in the car. He could not have survived it because the passenger side of my car was crushed and bent in half. I am grateful to God for this blessing.

I haven't seen Maurice since my accident, but one day Coach Jackson brought the football players to my hospital room. He told me how distressed Maurice was, and that he couldn't bear to visit. He also told Maurice that I would understand, and he was right. Maurice soon dropped out of high school, but he found his way back. He ultimately received his GED, and played college football in Arkansas. I like to think I helped him along the way.

It was a big day for all of us when the medical staff was finally able to get me out of the ICU and into a hospital room. They felt I was stabilized enough, and although there was still much to do, I was ready for the next phase. Mom was choking back tears when they moved me because she knew this was a big step forward. I had made it this far.

When you're in the hospital, they don't let you sleep a long time. For me, the doctors were so concerned about blood infections, changes in enzymes, internal bleeding and bruising, how my kidneys and liver were responding, and a long list of other possible complications that they had the nurses take blood every three or four hours every day no matter what. I also had to be rolled over every few hours to prevent bedsores, so it seemed like every time I fell asleep for five minutes, there was a nurse at my side pushing on me to wake up. I finally learned to just stretch out my arm and let them fill however many vials of blood they needed. It became so commonplace that I was almost able to sleep through it. Almost.

My pain never abated while I was at Forrest General, and on one occasion I spiked a frightful fever. They weren't sure I would live through the night, and the nursing staff was in a panic. The doctor ordered them to fill my bed with ice to help bring the fever down, and it worked. My head was burning up and my body was freezing, but I survived. For me, it was just another day in the hospital.

There is great indignity in being helpless in a hospital—perhaps even more so for a young man who prided himself on his physical strength and independence as I did. There was almost nothing I could do on my own, and I felt shame to have people feed me, bathe me, help me with bathroom needs, and turn me over in bed every couple of hours. I had built my life and my psyche on being strong and self-reliant, and all that died on the day of the accident. My sense of manhood, machismo, and physical strength was shattered in an instant, and it would take years to rebuild. Emotions boiled up inside me, and I wasn't equipped to deal with them all.

I had many hard lessons to learn about humility and how to graciously accept the help that others gave with love in their hearts.

"Get that food away from me," I said angrily, and I slapped it out of my mother's hand with the one arm that still worked. I was tired. I was depressed. I was embarrassed. And mostly I felt I was a burden on everyone when I was supposed to be the man. I was supposed to be helping other people, not lying helpless on a bed unable to eat a bite of food without spilling it on myself. I hated the hospital food anyway, and I had lost a lot of weight and strength because I had been on IV feeding for many days. I was frustrated that I couldn't do anything, and I hated it. I hated the pity I got, and I hated having people stare at me all the time. I tried valiantly to put others at ease and be the least burden I could possibly be, but I didn't always succeed. Sometimes, I just couldn't.

"Now, Dwight, this is a trial. It's a test of character, and if there's one thing you've got in bunches, it's character," Mom said. "God loves you, and he has a plan for you. You have to trust it."

"This is some plan, Mom. He might have gone about it a bit differently," I snapped back, my voice dripping with self-pity and anger.

"You're alive," she said. "And you may not feel it right now, but you have many blessings. You have a family that loves you and won't let you down. You have friends at your side every day because you worked to build those friendships over the years. You have a keen mind, and it won't be easy, but you're going to have a beautiful life. You have to trust."

Mom is a devout Christian, and she wouldn't let me turn away from God. But she did confess to me on one occasion that she questioned God on the day of the accident and wrote about it in her diary. She kept a journal of her thoughts and feelings every day I was in the hospital and during the two months I spent later on in rehab.

But she told me, "Dwight, I put those questions aside because God knows best. You'll come out of this stronger and better than ever, and you're showing us every day what true courage is all about." There was no messing with my mother. When she latched onto a point, she would clench it like a pit bull with a bone. I had learned long ago not to argue even if I was not where she was in believing that I had the courage or strength to handle what God had planned.

It's hard to resist a mother like this who won't accept defeat or self-pity. She knew everything I was going through, and it pained her every minute to see me struggle. I actually believe in many ways she was in more pain than I was. She just had the wisdom and experience to put a better face on it, and she filled me every day with positive thoughts and hope for the future. She can be hard to take sometimes, but she's impossible to resist.

Mom was there constantly. She had taken off work with her company's blessing and was in my room directing traffic and speaking with the doctors and updating visitors every day. And my friends and other members of my family visited often, too. Tamika, a fellow teacher, was there every day when I was in the ICU and most days when I was in the hospital room. Fellow church members from the New Hopewell Missionary Baptist Church in Taylorsville were there all the time, and I loved them for it. They lifted my spirits and brought me hope. They kept me updated on church and community concerns, and they were my local news service. The nurses in the ICU and later on in the hospital room would joke that I must be the most popular guy in Mississippi. There were always people there, and they would not let go of me.

I had many visitors during my time at Forrest General, but none more memorable than a beautiful lady who walked slowly into my room one day and just looked me up and down. Then she started talking.

"Dwight, my name is Pamela, and I want to tell you a story. A while back a reckless driver crashed into my vehicle, and I suffered grievous injuries. Almost every bone in my body was broken. It happened on Highway 84 near the same stretch where you had your accident. I couldn't be angry about things because I was unconscious and in a coma for the longest time. In fact, I was in a coma so long that the doctors said I was beginning to decay from the inside.

"I was on life support and couldn't breathe on my own," Pamela went on. "There was little hope that I would survive, and there was talk about taking me off of life support. My family wouldn't let it happen, and then one day I opened my eyes. I went through months and months of unforgiving pain, rehab, and soul searching. I went through every emotion you could feel. And I finally learned to accept the situation and work through it to make myself better. I'm here to tell you the biggest risk you face isn't a severed spine or paralysis. It's loss of hope. Son, you have a future in front on you, and you're responsible for it. I've heard a lot about you these past three weeks, and you are admired and loved. You can get through this and be an inspiration to others. Or you can quit. It's your call." Then she went quietly away.

By the time she was done, I was sobbing. I had fought my emotions so hard for so long, it seemed they could no longer be contained. Here was a lady giving me lessons in courage and strength. Her story was similar to mine, but mine was just beginning. She gave me hope. She gave me tough love. She challenged me to face my situation like a man. And above all, she gave me inspiration. By the time she left that day, I knew I could face the future. I wouldn't let myself give up, and I wouldn't give in to depression or anger. God had sent me my very own angel.

One day during my stay, my brothers and a couple of friends came by to visit. They were talking about Herman Posey, the drunk driver who slammed into my car. The conversation was a bit rough.

"We've got to put that rat bastard away for the rest of his useless life," said my older brother Cedrick, and everybody seemed to agree. "He hasn't called to see how you're doing. He hasn't whispered a word of apology. He couldn't care less," Cedrick said. We all knew we couldn't undo the accident. Maybe the next best thing was to exact revenge in the name of justice.

I had thought long and hard about Posey, and along the way my emotions ran the gamut from hatred to compassion to forgiveness. It was an emotional journey I travelled quickly with several setbacks along the way, but I understood one thing from hearing Pamela's story. Going forward, I had to focus on me. I had to regain strength and learn to become as self-reliant as possible. Every minute I spent thinking about Posey was a minute lost in my recovery. I couldn't afford hatred no matter how tempting it was. I couldn't afford negative thoughts. I had to battle them and keep them as far away from me as possible, and I knew that was my best chance to get better. It may sound honorable and big-hearted to let go of the hatred and forgive Posey for his actions, but I knew it was really for me. It was my only path forward.

"Yeah, Posey's bad news," I said. "It's hard to say anything good about him. But I'm the one in this hospital bed, and I'm the one who needs all your help. I'll never get better if we think about him instead of me. The state will deal with Posey, and we need to let this go." Everybody sat quietly but soon murmured their agreement. They weren't sure I was right, but they were willing to accept my verdict. Over time it became clear that I had made the right call because I needed to focus all my mental and physical energy on getting better, not on getting even.

Through most of my time at Forrest General, I suffered from severe internal bleeding. I couldn't see it, but it was there. After almost three weeks, the doctors decided I had to have a blood transfusion in part to prepare for my upcoming spinal surgery. My hemoglobin was way below acceptable levels, and they couldn't proceed without the transfusion.

It was awful. I already had a pick tube connected to my body, so they used that to do the transfusion. As soon as the blood started flowing into my body, I got a warming sensation all over me that lasted for the two hours of the transfusion. That was fine, but I could actually taste the blood in my mouth. It was bitter…nasty…disgusting. It was creepy. I hated the taste, and it stuck with me throughout the procedure and well into the next day. It was a surreal experience I hope never to repeat. But it was also necessary to prepare me for the major spinal cord surgery planned for two days later.

After three weeks at Forrest General, my two attending doctors, Dr. Donald and Dr. Wiebe, finally decided to operate on my severed spine. The delay was not the hospital's fault; it was their good judgment. I had experienced so many complications up to that point that they thought I might not survive the surgery. It had to happen sooner or later, however, and now was the time.

My spinal surgery occurred on August 25, 2005, three days before Hurricane Katrina hit the Gulf Coast. My two surgeons were as professional and informative as they could be. They explained what needed to be done, why they needed to do it, and the possible complications. It was a huge deal, and it would last many hours. We all knew there was a lot riding on it, and if I didn't have the operation, I would never be able to sit up, use my arms to transfer from place to place such as from a wheelchair to a bed, or brush my own teeth. I would be mostly—if not entirely—prone and basically have to stay in a reclining position forever. That was unacceptable, and no matter the risk, I wanted the surgery.

The staff rolled me off the bed and onto the gurney, and I remember the wheels clattering as we made our way to the operating room. Dr. Donald and Dr. Wiebe were already waiting there. They exuded an air of friendship and competence, and I knew that whatever happened, they would do right by me. The anesthesiologist delivered the medicine that knocked me out, and I lost consciousness immediately. I didn't even get a chance to count backwards from ten. The surgery lasted a grueling seven hours, but I didn't know it. When I regained consciousness, I was back in my room almost as if nothing had happened. I felt a new pain in my back, however—and by this time I considered myself an expert on the subject of pain. This new pain radiated throughout my body, like a stinger that football players sometimes get. If I moved ever so slightly the wrong way, the pain would flash across my torso. The doctors explained that this was expected and actually a good thing. The surgery had gone perfectly, and they were beyond pleased with the results. I would be, too…but not just yet.

They didn't waste any time letting me recover after surgery. They didn't want my back to stiffen, which would only complicate my recovery, so they started a rehab process within two days. I had lain flat for the past three weeks, and now they wanted to get me in a sitting position. I was in a bed with electric controls, so the doctors and therapists could elevate the head section ever so slowly, bit by bit. The pain was agonizing—beyond anything I could have imagined. I almost screamed, but managed to control myself. The therapy was necessary, and despite my protests, they kept at it. The doctors felt for me, but they knew if they didn't do it, it would be far worse in the long run.

Within two days, I reached the point where I could almost sit upright in bed, and it gave me a sense of freedom and self-reliance I hadn't known for weeks. Tamika was quick to praise my accomplishment.

"Dwight, now you can watch all the sports programs you want sitting up. Isn't that every man's dream?" We all laughed and enjoyed the moment.

At first, sitting up was dizzying and I was queasy from the change in position, a common occurrence after being prone for so long. But now, I could brush my own teeth, wash most of my body myself, feed myself, and move with greater freedom. It was exhilarating and brought me a fresh sense of optimism. This was the first time I actually saw a ray of hope that I would be able to do things on my own, and I was ready to face the shoulder surgery scheduled for the next day.

"Bring it on," I thought with a renewed sense of confidence.

One more surgery to go. Finally, after all these weeks of sharp, biting pain in my shoulder, they were going to take care of my torn rotator cuff. I would have the surgery on August 30, and I couldn't wait. But neither could Katrina.

Hurricane Katrina hit with ferocity and vengeance. It lashed out with an angry voice and an iron fist, and it demolished countless buildings and destroyed many lives.

For me, it was a blessing in disguise, but I didn't know it at the time.

The wind howled outside my room like a train passing by…only it kept on and on. Rain pelted my windows and the sides of the hospital. The noise was deafening, the sky was black, and the scene was frightening. It seemed like the end of time.

It went from bad to worse when the hospital lost electrical power, and then the back-up generators were destroyed as well. The hospital was in a panic, and many of the staff wanted to leave to go protect their own families. We were unattended with no power and no light. Just the howling wind and the pounding rain. It was a scene from a horror movie. After a day of this, the hospital ordered an evacuation of all patients. They moved everybody into the hallways, but we still couldn't leave. The hurricane's fury didn't abate until the next day, and then there were so many fallen trees and downed power lines on the roads that the ambulances couldn't go anywhere. The hospital was stifling without ventilation, and it got harder and harder for me to breathe. My mom had to stand over me hour after hour, fanning me to keep me cool. When one arm got exhausted, she would switch to the other. Her only break was to get towels every so often to wipe the sweat off me and cool the rest of my body. We spent two days in torturous conditions before they could start moving people out. We lived on warm water, potato chips, and graham crackers, and we all knew I couldn't survive in these circumstances much longer.

When they finally started evacuating the patients, they removed the people in most danger first. By then, the hospital considered me toward the middle of the pack in terms on my condition, so I kept waiting my turn. I waited and waited, and my attending nurse got angrier and angrier as she and my mom noticed people in better condition than me leaving the hospital. Mom finally couldn't take it any longer, and she went to the temporary trailers outside where the hospital administration had set up shop.

"You can put me in jail right now, but you are gonna get my son out of this hospital this very minute," she told the staff member and the police officer standing next to her. "He is paralyzed and on death's doorstep, and you're taking out people with nothing worse than a stubbed toe. You get up there right now and put him in an ambulance," she said with tears streaming down her face. The head nurse was with my Mom and vouched for everything she said. Mom later told me that she was ready to drag people up to my room if necessary because she didn't know what else to do. It worked. They went there right away and started preparing me for the trip to the Methodist Rehabilitation Center about ninety miles away in Jackson, Mississippi.

I say this was a blessing for me because the Methodist Rehabilitation Center was the finest in the state, perhaps in the country, and they were always filled to capacity. They would have been too crowded to accept me under normal circumstances, but this was not a normal circumstance. I had nowhere else to go, and they had to take me even though I wasn't ready for rehab yet because I still needed surgery on my rotator cuff. But take me they did, and I soon began the next chapter in my journey to recovery.

Katrina was devastating. I, perhaps, am the only person in the world who owes a debt of gratitude to that monstrous hurricane. Katrina took me right where I needed to go, and my life began to change dramatically for the better in its aftermath.

6

THE GRIND

I t was magical. I had not seen daylight or felt a breeze on my face for almost a month, but now I was outside breathing fresh air, feeling the wind blow gently over me, and basking in sunlight. I didn't know how much I had missed it all, and I couldn't help but smile. I heard dogs barking in the distance and saw squirrels darting from place to place. Even though I could only enjoy it all for a few minutes before they placed me in the ambulance, it was wonderful to be alive and witness the world around me. Mom, of course, had started her car and was ready to follow the ambulance. The trip from Forrest General to the Methodist Rehabilitation Center in Jackson was a great change of pace, almost like a student field trip.

The EMTs loaded me into the ambulance, and I quickly noticed that it had a couple of small windows I could peek through. It was a gift, and as we got underway, I saw much of the damage Katrina had left in her wake. Telephone lines knocked down, roofs ripped off of houses, trees strewn everywhere. It was a shock, but it was also my first exposure to the outside world for a long while, and I drank it all in. Nurse Kathy was with me on the trip, and she told me about the looting, about people siphoning gas from others' cars, and about the devastation along the coast and in Louisiana. She also told me about the courage many showed in helping others in dire circumstances, about the efforts the National Guard and others made to search for survivors, and about the community joining hands to meet a common challenge.

The drive lasted about two hours and was generally uneventful. Nurse Kathy watched the road closely and would often lean over and hold me as we approached a bumpy stretch so I would not move in unexpected ways. With my broken back, torn rotator cuff, and other injuries still squawking, even the slightest movement in the wrong direction was painful. I was profoundly grateful to have her at my side then, and I made sure she knew it. I was even more grateful for the warmth and empathy she had shown throughout my time at Forrest General. The only thing greater than her skills was her heart.

When we arrived in Jackson, they were expecting us. Much of the paperwork had already been prepared, although they still needed some more details and wanted my signature on several documents far too lengthy and complex for me to absorb at that time. There was, of course, one major problem. When the nurses saw me and read through my medical history, I heard them speaking among themselves.

"He shouldn't be here. He still needs surgery on his shoulder," said one nurse.

"We can't start rehab until that's done," another agreed. "He's not ready."

Fortunately, the rehab center is physically connected to the hospital, and the operation on my shoulder was scheduled for two days after my arrival. Finally.

In a way, I was glad I had to wait two days for the surgery. Moving to any new environment is stressful, and I didn't know what to expect in rehab. I did know that it would test me in many ways, and I wasn't sure I was completely ready yet. During those two days, I had a chance to observe how they went about the rehab process, see quadriplegics and other people with neck and spinal injuries in even worse shape than I was, and generally get the lay of the land. This helped me prepare mentally and put myself in the right frame of mind for the grind that lay ahead. I also met Ryan the first day I arrived.

Ryan Estep had been admitted to rehab a few weeks before I arrived. His spine had been severed in a car accident that occurred in the same week as mine. There was no drunk driver involved in his case, but he wasn't wearing his seatbelt, and that changed his life forever. One small lapse in judgment, and he is now paying a price that will last the rest of his life.

Ryan was entering his senior year in high school and was a great athlete. He was a young man with boundless energy and infectious enthusiasm. I am about five years older than Ryan, but when he learned that a fellow football player and high school football coach was in rehab, he wheeled his way to my room in record time.

"Hey, Coach. I'm Ryan. I brought you some Gushers, my favorite candy. Doesn't mean we can hold hands or anything, and I'm real sorry you're here, but I'm glad you're here too," he said without taking a breath. It was friendship at first sight, and we spent the next five weeks side-by-side working together in rehab, urging each other on, and getting into a little mischief now and again—usually initiated by Ryan. We are close friends to this day.

Ryan came to terms very quickly with his situation, and he would greet and help new arrivals get accustomed to the goings on at rehab. He was quick with a smile, loved a prank, and was full of healthy competition. When I learned that he was the star running back at his high school, I told him I used to tackle running backs like him during my high school days. It was my favorite thing to do back then.

"Ryan, you may be good, but you'd be running in the other direction when you saw me coming for you," I said with a grin.

And he promptly replied, "Damn, Coach. All you'd be able to do is rub the dust out of your eyes when I went running past you."

Like me, Ryan was one of only two or three football players to play both sides of the ball in our respective high schools. He was a running back on offense and a free safety on defense. It was clear he was a gifted athlete and, in fact, he still is. I quickly realized that Ryan had a sharp wit and wisdom far beyond his years. We had a lot to talk about.

After meeting with Ryan and learning some more about rehab protocols, I felt ready for the next phase. Two days later, I was back on the gurney, my primary mode of transportation, and heading to the operating room for my shoulder surgery. The rehab staff rolled me next door for the operation, and I was excited. Surgeries seemed commonplace at that point…but this one promised to be my last. I was eager to get it behind me. I had been waiting for this a long time.

I wasn't the least bit concerned until the surgery actually started. I was supposed to receive anesthesia to make the operation painless. I did, but it wasn't. They injected me with the wrong anesthesia, and I felt every slice and every twitch during the operation. I almost screamed out in anguish because it was so painful, but I knew it would end, and I knew I could tough it out. This was my final surgery, or so I thought, and I had lots of first-hand experience with pain. I could work through a little more. I was grateful beyond words when it was over, and I was hopeful that this was my last visit to an operating room.

The rehab center wasn't really ready for me because I wasn't ready for them. I still had to recover from my shoulder surgery; my breathing was labored and inadequate; the doctors were fearful of infections and blood clots; and my broken ribs, broken back, and many internal injuries had not healed sufficiently to withstand a rigorous rehab regimen. But I was there—and they had to deal with me the way they found me. I didn't care. I felt I could work through the pain and would benefit from their expertise.

For most of my time in Forrest General, I understood that I was paralyzed…or, I should say, I sort of understood it. I couldn't move my legs, which was a pretty big clue. But I still had pain in them all the time. It's called phantom pain, like when an amputee can still feel pain in his leg even after it's been cut off. In my mind, I could grasp the concept of paralysis, but nothing the doctor said made it seem completely real. I didn't feel it in my soul. It seemed surreal that I had to lie prone on my bed all the time, virtually every minute of every day, until the final two days I was at Forrest General. I couldn't even lift myself up because of my severed spine and fractured back. All that changed quite suddenly the day after my shoulder surgery.

"Dwight, we need to put you in the wheelchair," said the nurse. Up to that point, whenever I had been transported, I was lying down on a gurney. They would roll me from one place to the next. I hadn't really considered any other alternative. I would listen to the wheels clatter unevenly as I got pushed along, and it came to feel natural. Now, without warning, they wanted me in a chair. I was caught off guard and more than a little scared.

All I could come up with in protest was a guttural "Huh?"

They gently lifted me out of bed and placed me in the wheelchair. I had to sit up straight, and the pain stabbed through my torso. It was excruciating. I was instantly dizzy and nauseated. My circulation had gotten so poor from having been prone for so long that I had a terrible reaction to sitting up suddenly.

"I'm gonna throw up," I told the doctor, a sense of panic washing over me. The doctor calmly explained that this was normal and that everybody had the same reaction when they got into the wheelchair for the first time after having lain flat for a long period of time. He said the nausea would pass and that this was a critical step in my recovery. It did pass, but not right away, and I can still feel the dizzying, nauseating sensation of vertigo, much like taking a sudden drop on a roller coaster.

Until that moment, I hadn't fully understood that I was paralyzed. And now, all of a sudden, through the fog of pain and nausea, it all came together. It hit me in a flash, and my mind felt as paralyzed as my body. I finally understood. This was my new reality. This was my new life.

Wheelchairs are tricky things, and they take a lot of getting used to. During rehab, the doctors generally want people to use a manual chair, which forces them to use their arms to propel themselves along. This builds arm strength and endurance, and both are critical for people in my situation. But since I had just undergone rotator cuff surgery, I was forced to use a power chair. At first, I was fearful of tipping over, the worst situation of all for somebody who's paralyzed. I didn't realize how fast the thing could go, and when I pressed the button to go forward, it was like pressing on a car's accelerator. The chair jerked forward abruptly. Controlling the speed while staying on course at the same time took far more practice than I'd imagined. But most of all, I was afraid of banging into things—counters, walls, chairs, other people in wheelchairs. I banged into walls on more than one occasion, especially when I tried to back up or turn around in tight spaces, and the staff started joking with me about it.

"Dwight, we're gonna have to hire a sheetrock crew," or "Are you sure you didn't play ice hockey? The concept is to avoid the walls, not crash into them!" It was all part of the process, and the staff knew I would get the hang of it soon enough.

Another problem was that with a severed spine, I often didn't know when I had hit something. I wouldn't feel it if I was concentrating on something else, such as not crashing into the nurse coming down the hallway, and I felt no sensation of pain from the contact. The circulation in my legs is degraded, a condition that can rapidly turn small problems into big ones. Small blisters and bruises become major oozing sores requiring rounds of IV antibiotics and medical intervention, all of which would delay my rehab. But still I knew I could master that mechanical monster, and once I did, it would offer freedom and mobility. I just needed to learn its ways and tame the beast first.

I didn't get long to rest after the surgery on my left shoulder because, as painful as it was, the rehab center had to start my shoulder rehab before I could get into the broader therapy program for my spine. They were relentless. Professional in every respect, their driving philosophy was "tough love," with emphasis on the "tough" part.

Two days after the surgery, Mary, my primary physical therapist, said, "Dwight, we're about to start a relationship," and she began pulling and stretching my left arm in ways that seemed unholy. It reminded me of pictures I had seen of people on the rack, during the Middle Ages, having all their limbs pulled in different directions. Mary raised my arm as high as it could possibly go, and then she raised it a little higher for good measure; she rotated it vigorously; she stretched it up and down; and she ignored my every protest. The pain was searing, and Mary knew it. I cried out and tears welled in my eyes, but she knew the pain would pass. She said I just had to work through it.

"Now, Dwight, a big strong football player like yourself should be able to handle a little nuisance pain," she chided.

"Nuisance pain, my ass," I said, partly in jest, but mostly in anger. She understood. She smiled. But she kept on going. She was incredible, a professional's professional. And my pain wasn't a big concern; my recovery was.

My "dates" with Mary went on day after day, and I began to dream of ways to get out them. I knew I had to go on, however, and I never backed out, no matter how tempted I was.

"Mary, you're in my dreams you know," I told her. "And not in a good way."

She just laughed and said, "I have that effect on a lot of people."

During the next week, I finally began to get some strength and flexibility back in my arm. The process was torturous, and I hated it, but it was working. My arm and tendons were stretched every morning. But there was no choice, and Mary expected nothing but my full cooperation. She often laughed with me.

"You keep fightin' me on this and I'm gonna tell your mama. See what she has to say," Mary would often joke. She dared me. She pushed me. She called me a big baby and a goof. And she made all the difference in the world. She prepared me in record time for the even more extensive rehab that lay ahead.

Primary rehab was in the morning at the center, and then I was largely left to my own devices for the rest of the day. I went from the arm and shoulder rehab to breathing rehab, which I hated almost as much. As I did at Forrest General, I had to breathe as deeply as possible and exhale as much air as I could into an electronic tube. They measured the strength and volume of my breathing, and it was still weak. For over two months I had to do breathing therapy twice a day every day except Sunday for about fifteen to twenty minutes each time. It was exhausting. In addition, they still had to take a blood sample every three or four hours like they did at Forrest

General and roll me over to prevent bedsores. An uninterrupted night's sleep was simply not in the cards.

Ryan was in and out of my room at various points every day, and we would often hang out in the rec room. He would speed down the hallway as fast as he could, trying to leave rubber marks on the floor.

"Hey, Coach, what's doin'?" he asked. "You know that pretty nurse that spends most of her time on the computer? I'm gonna ask her to take a ride with me on the wheelchair and pop a wheelie. Whaddaya think?"

Ryan always found a way to make the best of things, and he was always looking for a reason to laugh. He was a great patient, and the rehab staff loved him.

While Ryan was also paralyzed from the waist down, his spine was severed farther down the spinal cord at T-12. This meant he could use his stomach muscles and had a little extra range of motion. Miraculously, he had suffered no additional injuries in his crash, even though his vehicle had flipped over a couple of times, and he was able to start rehab right after his accident. I had to go forward at a much slower pace, and I was annoyed at my lack of progress.

"You'll be fine, Coach. You have arms like I-beams, and once you get started, you'll be making progress in no time at all," he said encouragingly. He made me smile every time he came by, and over time, we developed a profound admiration for each other. We talked football all the time, and it helped pass the hours. Who were the Heisman hopefuls this year? What teams were most likely to win the SEC? Who had the best defense? Ryan had grown up in Louisiana and was a big LSU Tigers fan. I, of course, would pull for Mississippi teams, knowing full well that they were big underdogs. We watched TV together and would just hang out. He made me feel better, and that helped him as well. I knew I could learn a great deal from his enthusiastic spirit and positive attitude. Ryan was not going to let a little thing like a severed spine get in his way.

Once my shoulder had healed enough, I started joining the larger group for spinal cord therapy every morning after shoulder and breathing therapy. This therapy, of course, could do nothing to repair our spinal cords. Once a spinal cord is severed, the body is forever paralyzed from that point down. End of story. But there is still the possibility of learning skills to make life better.

We would work in groups of two or sometimes three people and rotate from one workstation to the next. For example, at one station, we would try to sit up straight for as long as possible—which was not very long in the beginning. There were two problems. It was painful keeping a straight posture, and my sense of balance was distorted. Since you have no control of your legs when you're paralyzed, balance is a very tricky thing—you can't use your legs to counterbalance the weight of your torso. Initially, I couldn't sit up long without tilting and then falling to one side. It seemed almost comical, like something from a sitcom on TV. The physical therapist would catch me, and we would do the drill again. And then again. And again. This helped build up strength and endurance in my back, which are essential for a paralyzed person. It also helped improve my sense of balance and build confidence as I got better and better over time. After I was strong enough to sit up for a while and keep my balance, the therapists would gently throw dodge balls at me. Even the slightest unexpected motion could tip me over. But this was all part of the therapy. In a few weeks, I became so skilled that they couldn't knock me over no matter how hard they threw the ball. Soon enough, we were having competitions throwing the ball as hard as possible back and forth to each other, and it became a fun part of the day. We would trash talk back and forth. I'd ask the therapist, "Is that all you got? I'll knock you over before you knock me over if you can't throw it any harder." I enjoyed the camaraderie, and it almost seemed like an athletic event.

Another one of the rotations was designed to help me keep my balance while moving in the wheelchair. It involved cones set up on the floor that were similar to but smaller than the ones you see on highways. I would have to roll the wheelchair manually and then lean over and pick up the cones without tipping over. It sounds easy enough, but it was scary in the beginning. It was hard to look at the floor, keep the chair rolling, and move my body weight without losing control. Sometimes I would spin out of control and knock the cones over instead of picking them up. Of course this always evoked a comment from the therapist.

"Damn, Dwight. How'd you ever get a driver's license in the first place? You know, you're making me look bad, and I just asked for a raise," he joked.

As with everything else, this exercise got easier over time. After a few weeks, I could zoom through the course and do it in my sleep. I became less and less afraid of tipping over and was gaining confidence each day. It was a big step.

Another major step was learning "transfers": a critical skill that I had to pick up fast. "Transferring" means moving yourself from the wheelchair to a bed, a car, a toilet seat, or wherever you need to go—and then moving yourself back into the chair again. Without the use of my legs, I can't balance easily because I can't move my legs or place my feet naturally where they need to be. Instead, I had to learn to reach down and use my arms to move my legs to the right position so that I could use them for leverage. Also, when you transfer, you have to put all your weight on one arm of the wheelchair for an instant as you push up and make your jump from the chair to wherever you need to be. This puts you at risk of toppling over, which was my greatest fear. It seemed almost impossible at first because I thought the wheelchair would flip over when I put all my weight on one arm. I saw everybody doing it and knew I could too, but it seemed unnatural.

We practiced transfers for hours and hours. There was always a physical therapist by our side helping with technique and ready to catch us if we fell. And fall I did. Ryan was often nearby when I practiced transfers and would laugh or make some comment each time the therapist had to catch me.

"Dwight, you're too damn big to make that little fella catch you all the time. Hope he don't drop you," he would joke. Of course, the therapist never did.

It's relatively easy to transfer from the chair to something that's about the same height as the chair, but things don't always work that easily. Toilet and car seats can be lower or higher, so you also have to lift or drop yourself as you shift your weight. It took a lot of athleticism to develop this technique, and I was grateful for the skills I had learned on the football field. I'm also right-handed and find it easier and more natural to transfer to my right. However, I don't always have that luxury. I had to become equally adept at transferring to the left, because bathrooms in particular often have their transfer bars on the left as you enter the stall. Despite the great impact of the Americans with Disabilities Act, much of the world is not designed for people with disabilities. We have to be adaptable and learn to handle conditions however we find them.

During another rotation, we would do reps with weights to build up arm strength and endurance. I used a manual wheelchair during therapy because it forced me to exercise my arms as I rolled from place to place, which is a big part of the therapy regimen. In my case, this meant using my arms to propel 220 pounds of body weight around the room. Today, there are times when I go to the mall or other places and roll up to four miles in a couple of hours. That is grueling work, and it just can't be done without strong arms. In fact, people in wheelchairs often look strange because of this extra work for their upper bodies. If their spine was severed at T-10 or below, for example, they lose all control of their stomach muscles. That's why you often see people in wheelchairs with large stomachs but very powerful arms.

When we lifted weights, they were always quite light, typically five to ten pounds. This was because the rehab staff wanted us to lift for a long time to build endurance, but they also didn't want us to hurt ourselves. As football players used to lifting hundreds of pounds, this seemed like a joke to Ryan and me.

"Hey, Coach, why don't they just ask me to lift my socks? It would do about as much good," said Ryan. "I'm gonna take care of this," he added, and then quickly rolled off to find some real weights. He came back with two forty pounders, and the competition was on. "Coach, you were probably never as strong as me, so I'll spot you ten reps. Bet I can do more than you."

Of course, I knew this was outside rehab protocol, but a dare is a dare, and I couldn't just let it slide. I responded in kind. "Ryan, with your girly muscles, I doubt you can even curl these weights ten times, let alone spot me ten reps. I'll spot you twenty reps and we'll see how it goes. Loser buys pizza for dinner."

We were busted as soon as the therapists saw what we were up to. We complained that the weights they gave us were too light to do any good, but they wouldn't change their minds. Rules were rules. We did, however, manage to secure larger weights every now and then after therapy was done for the day, and Ryan and I were grateful to actually get a decent workout.

Ryan's great gift was spontaneity and a spirit that would never give in to despair. We would often sit side-by-side in the rec center, and he would suddenly tug on my arm and say something like, "Hey, Coach. Look at Debbie. She just gets prettier every day."

I would wince in pain because my shoulder still hurt from surgery and say, "Damn, Ryan. Quit yanking on my arm. I have enough to deal with without you adding to the problem."

Ryan would just laugh and say, "Sorry, Coach. Got a little excited. But you gotta admit, Debbie's a fine package." Ryan always made me smile, and he was instrumental in making rehab a bearable and even joyful experience. He helped show me the importance of sharing the best you have with other

people, and I came to realize just how essential a positive attitude can be…
But I also learned to position myself so he couldn't grab my left arm when he
had an inspired thought he needed to share.

I sometimes had visitors while going through rehab sessions, and Tamika,
my mom, and my brothers and sisters would often watch me on weekends.
It was an eye-opener for everybody to learn all the motor skills involved
in doing the most basic movements, things most of us take for granted.
They would gasp to see me tip over on the mat or spin out of control in the
wheelchair trying to pick up the cones, but then they would laugh to see
that I was smiling or laughing each time it happened. I even had them roll
around in the wheelchair so they could see what it was like and share in the
experience. They were learning more and more about how to deal with me,
and that too was an important part of the therapy.

I was one of the lucky ones at rehab because I had visitors there all
the time. My room at rehab was almost like a motel suite. It had a large
television, and it could accommodate many visitors and even an overnight
guest or two. This was a big step up from a normal hospital room. The center
encouraged visitors, and unlike standard hospitals, they were welcome at all
hours and treated like VIPs. They brought the outside world with them and
added energy to the rehab center. They lifted the spirits of the patients, and
they were good medicine. I had more visitors than I could count, and it was
a great gift in my life. My mother and Tamika, my brothers, sisters, aunts,
uncles, friends from school, my church family, my pastor, and many, many
others. They supported me at every turn and made sure I had reason to stay
on my rehab path. I think of these friends and relatives every day, and feel
gratitude in my heart for their love.

Mom was there every weekend, every holiday, and every spare moment
she could find. She and Tamika were a team. Talking, tending, preaching,
helping, encouraging, annoying. Mom did all the Mom things she was
supposed to do, and I loved her for it.

"Dwight, quit fussing about your breathing rehab," she said. "You're
being a goofball, and you just need to accept that that's how you're gonna
start your day. By the way, I got a call from Cedrick, and he plans to visit next
week. Here's a cake I brought from the church. Rocky seems to wonder
where you are."

Mom would pour everything out all at once, and then we could circle
back and revisit everything she said. My older brother Cedrick was in the

Navy, and it wasn't easy for him to get time off. I looked forward to seeing him, and we always had a good time together. Rocky was our pet Chihuahua, and I missed him greatly. Mom would talk and talk and then talk some more. Then she would sit quietly for a while—as if she needed to recharge her battery.

I never felt disconnected from family or community, and I became more and more aware of just how important it was to have people who loved me in my life. Whenever I felt sad or ready to call it quits, I knew I had to keep going. I couldn't let them down. Not everybody was as lucky as I was, and I knew it.

The rehab center was a place of great hope and optimism, but it was also a place of deep despair. The hope and optimism were firmly rooted in the center's many professionals, who offered the best treatment imaginable. The staff treated every patient as if they did not have a disability at all, and they expected top-notch performance from the patients and themselves alike. The doctors, nurses, psychiatrists, and physical and occupational therapists made sure everyone learned to become as independent and self-reliant as possible. They were with each patient every step of the way. They pushed everyone hard and then harder yet until the patients could do things they never thought they'd be able to do again. For me, this meant that the staff fed my spirit, tended my body, and encouraged me to do just one more rep, one more bend, one more everything. They also urged me to stay out of my room after therapy in the morning and to spend time in the recreation center, to eat lunch at one of the cafeterias instead of in my room, to visit with other patients, and to become as active as possible. As I learned new skills, they even took me to outside activities like wheelchair bowling, wheelchair tennis, and board skiing. They didn't accept "no" for an answer, and they taught me to push myself as hard as I could to get as far as I could. The Methodist Rehabilitation Center is a remarkable place, and it deserves every bit of the reputation it has earned across the country.

But at the same time, the center was filled with people facing obstacles that could at times seem insurmountable. People who could run five miles one day learned the next that they would never walk again. And they had to endure agonizing pain as an extra bonus. Some people were quadriplegics who had no use of their arms or legs, and they felt hopeless about their future. Others had families that simply couldn't stand the strain. Spouses left after many years of marriage, and family members stopped coming by to visit. It could be harsh, and depression was often the result.

Every patient there had a grievous injury, and they all went through many layers of emotion, often several times in the same day. Joy at having learned how to put on their own socks for the first time in months, anguish in accepting that this was now a great accomplishment. Anger at their situations; gratitude that they had loving families to help them though those situations.

All the patients were in a constant battle with their own psyches. The medical staff was expertly skilled at helping us cope with our emotions, which were every bit as gripping as our physical traumas. In a place like the rehab center, people learn a great deal about themselves—their courage, their stamina, their spirit, and their willingness to keep going no matter what. Not everybody does.

People who are recently disabled battle depression and often have thoughts of suicide. It goes with the territory. Paralysis is a grim and unexpected fate, and the psychological battles are as tough as the physical ones. The rehab center is keenly attuned to this, and the staff closely monitors the mental health and spirits of their patients. While I had my bad days and my good ones, I strove to fill my life with positive thoughts and enthusiastic people. I like to think the best of other people, take whatever comes in stride, and put the best possible face on any situation. Like all patients, I met with staff psychiatrists periodically, and they commended me for my attitude and perspective. Then they put me to work.

Often the best medicine for somebody with a grave injury is to spend time with another person in the same situation. The shared bonds of a common experience, similar goals and challenges, and the sense of fighting the same battle ease the path to recovery. The doctors often asked me to meet with new arrivals and counsel other people going through rehab. I like to help people, which is one reason I became a teacher, and I like to share my thoughts. I understood what the newcomers were going through, and I had already spent a great deal of time sorting out my own emotions. I would sit for hours with other people who had only just realized that their new best friend was their wheelchair, and we would share our stories. Mostly this meant sharing our feelings and our fears. How do we get through this? Will I be a burden on everybody for the rest of my life? Will my family leave me? How do I withstand this pain? We would encourage each other, keep track of each other's progress, celebrate our victories, and simply find solace in knowing that we were not alone. Over time, I became more concerned about the people around me than I was about myself. I would be pained by their setbacks and rejoice in their accomplishments. I didn't know it yet, but this was the best possible medicine for my own recovery. Perhaps most important of all, I learned that I wanted to devote myself to helping others in similar situations, and I promised God I would do just that going forward.

Not everybody is successful in rehab, and the hardest part for me was watching people who were thinking and talking about suicide. They didn't see a future for themselves. People can work through pain, but hopelessness is another matter. I would sometimes speak with my preacher and ask him how best to help these people. What wisdom and insight could he give to help me help them? If I was ever depressed during this very long ordeal, it was at those times when I couldn't help other people when they needed help the most.

I continued to improve in small steps. I remember the day I was first able to go through the buffet line at lunch—a huge accomplishment.

"Hey, Coach. Let's go to the buffet for lunch today," Ryan suggested. I paused for a moment because I had known this would come eventually, and I was more than a little concerned. I had not yet dared the buffet line, which meant balancing a plate that I couldn't feel on my lap, extending my arms to scoop the food, and rolling my wheelchair to the table after my plate was loaded. I envisioned the worst. I would bump into somebody or something; I would drop my plate. I just knew everything would end up on the floor. I had feared the day Ryan would make this suggestion.

"Okay, Ryan, let's do it," I answered with all the confidence I could muster. If this day had to come, it might as well be today.

We rolled ourselves down to the cafeteria and gave them our meal tickets that let us eat for free. Guests had to pay. I told Ryan to go first, and I watched his every move. He didn't know it, but he was teaching me an important skill. I saw exactly how he balanced his plate, how he scooped up the food, and how he kept everything on an even keel. When we got to the table, he said, "Coach, you did great. I really struggled my first time, but you didn't miss a beat."

"Now, Ryan," I joked, "that's because I'm super coordinated."

Ryan just looked at me oddly for a second and said, "Coach, you're many things, but super coordinated isn't one of them. I think you did this before and didn't tell me," he laughed.

It was another step, and I felt great.

Things, however, never go perfectly, and I suffered a severe setback about a month into my rehab. I was still battling internal injuries and constant pain, and I came down with an allergic reaction to a new medication that caused my fever to spike to a dangerous level. I had to stop rehab for a few days, and this annoyed me even more than the illness itself. Back on IV antibiotics. Stuck in bed with no strength or energy to do anything. I was afraid that I would slip backward and lose what progress I had made so far. I had earned each little success along the way, and I didn't want to have to start over.

Ryan was getting ready to leave rehab at that point because he had been there almost two months and was ready to move on. Of course, he stopped by my room before leaving and weighed in with his thoughts in his own inimitable way.

"Coach, don't be a dope. You've been showing us all how to do this rehab thing. You won't miss a beat."

To Ryan's great credit, he could call me a dope, and I would somehow feel good about it. I was happy that he had completed his rehab and was ready to move on, but I knew I would miss spending time with him every day. He had been a huge help to me and to others, and it was a sad day. When I mentioned this, Ryan just took it in stride.

"Coach, you're not getting rid of me that easily. I'll be back soon enough. We still have to do a wheelie contest. And," he added, "when I get back, I'll be driving here on my own."

And that's exactly what happened. Ryan returned a few weeks later all pumped up and proud of his new set of wheels. He had completed a special driver's training course, received his certification from Mississippi State University, and had all the necessary equipment installed in his vehicle. He was going places on his own, and he said being able to drive gave him freedom to do everything. He was proud as could be, and we all rolled down to the parking lot to inspect his new chariot. I felt his exuberance and sense of accomplishment, and it gave me a new goal to shoot for.

After recovering from my allergic reaction, it was back to the rehab floor every morning. To my great relief, I picked up right where I had left off. By this time, I was able to maneuver my wheelchair like a pro, and I could lean over and pick up cones at a swift pace. I no longer feared falling over and was ready for the next challenge. So were the therapists.

I and the other patients learned to work with a gripper so we could extend our reach and pick things up off the floor, from countertops, and out of cabinets. This is an important skill, and it's not nearly as easy as it sounds. When I started to get a handle on it, the therapist dumped a bucket of small items all over the floor and said, "Okay, Dwight. I want all that stuff picked up and back in the bucket when I get back in twenty minutes." It seemed a little cruel, but it was great exercise. We had to pick up pennies, nails, tacks, tiny pills, marbles, and slippery little things. Something the size of a wallet is simple, but pills and pennies are tough. It was frustrating and annoying, and it would often take a full half hour to get everything back in the bucket. It was good for me all the same, and it gave me more independence and a great boost of confidence. When the therapist came back, he would usually say something like, "That was too easy! Next time I'll have to give you a real challenge."

There were many patients in rehab, and most of us had similar injuries. Many were in much worse shape than I was because they had broken necks, which meant they had no motion or feeling at all from the neck down. They couldn't use their arms or legs, and the path ahead of them was going to be very difficult. It broke my heart to see what they went through, but it also made me realize that I was lucky to have severed my spine where I did. I was gaining greater strength and flexibility in my arms by the day, and I was becoming more and more self-reliant. That, after all, is the ultimate goal of rehab.

Joey was one of everyone's favorite patients in rehab. We called him "The Vet" because he had been in a wheelchair for the past fifteen years. He was back because he needed some therapy on his legs, but he knew all the tricks and had all the answers. He was our source of knowledge, and we hounded him mercilessly with questions.

"Joey, what's it like when you drive? Are you scared?"

"Joey, will I ever be able to have sex again?" This was a huge question on everyone's mind.

Joey laughed and said, "The short answer is 'yes'". You can have a full and fun sex life, but you'll have to learn a few things along the way. Like rehab, it's not necessarily easy in the beginning, but you'll be plenty motivated and learn everything you need to know in short order." Of course, we were all relieved to hear this answer.

"Joey, how do you get used to people staring at you all the time? Does it still bother you?"

"Joey, what was the hardest thing to get used to when you got out of rehab?"

"Joey, do you still do personal rehab at home?"

On and on, and Joey showed remarkable patience. He answered our questions fully and prompted us to think of many others. He was a great resource, and everybody wanted to hear his wisdom, learn his tricks of the trade, and sit next to him during lunch.

It was important during rehab to socialize and not just go back to my room to rest after the various exercises in the morning. And there was a lot to do. A group of us would hang out in somebody's room and watch TV or play video games. We had long sessions playing card games like hearts or spades. We would have pizza parties to celebrate a milestone somebody had reached, and we would often roll down to the cafeteria together to have lunch as a group. The recreation center was our gathering place, and we would play board games like Monopoly or Scrabble, have dart tournaments, or go outside the center itself and get some fresh air. We knew every morning would include a rigorous workout, but the afternoons and evenings were fun times. Our muscles and our spirits would renew themselves and get a little stronger each day. We developed a sense of camaraderie and fellowship, and we would always help each other out when the going got especially tough.

I'm a social person and enjoyed being with other people, but I also need my private time. I found this on the balcony.

On the second floor of the rec center, there was a balcony that overlooked much of Jackson. I could sit there and see the city spread itself out before me. It was a popular place to talk in small groups or just sit and think. I liked to bring visitors there to chat, or I'd just spend time there alone gathering my thoughts. We all found comfort on the balcony, and it was a refuge for my spirit.

One day my preacher, Reverend Evans, came by to visit. He had visited before and was keeping close tabs on my progress so he could report back to my church family. His timing was perfect because I had been struggling a bit in recent days. For all its virtues, rehab was a relentless process, and I was still in pain every day. I still had phantom pain in my legs, which was every bit as distressing as real pain. I had pain in my shoulder from the surgery and from constantly pushing my arms to the limit, pain in my chest from my broken ribs, and pain in my heart at the thought of living in a wheelchair forever. Could I ever be really independent? Could I ever fall in love? Would a woman ever be able to love me? Could I have a family and know the joy of raising children? I was usually upbeat, but sometimes the weight of it all landed on my heart with the same impact my car had when it struck the tree. During these moments I would sit alone at night on the balcony and try to make sense of it all. Sometimes I would just pray.

Reverend Evans is a wise man, and he had been a big part of my life. He had ministered at the New Hopewell Missionary Baptist Church for over twenty-five years at that point—longer than my lifetime. He was a force in the community, and he was respected and loved in many quarters. He listened patiently with love in his heart.

"Dwight, I want you to write a letter to God," he said. "Tell him your fears and what's on your mind. Tell him your hopes and dreams for the future. Think hard about it, and write it all down. Then keep a copy of the letter and give me one. I'll bet a year from now you'll see that this was all a test, and you had the courage and strength of character to pass with flying colors."

I considered Reverend Evans's words and spent hours and hours thinking about the assignment. Then I went to work. I wrote my letter, and I asked God for the strength to make it through rehab. I asked him to show me the way to help other people in similar situations. I asked him to help me get back my independence. And, finally, I asked him to let me find love in my life. I figured if I was going to ask for something, I might as well ask for it all.

Rehab continued largely without incident. I got stronger and stronger, and to my great delight, my breathing finally returned to normal after almost three months. Rehab had been the most physically difficult, painful, and psychologically trying time of my life. I learned that there were things in me that I'd never imagined, and I gained the confidence to face life head-on. Not only that, I became inspired to be a positive force for those around me. It was the end of October 2005, and it was time to leave.

7

A BRIGHT LIGHT

I have been blessed with many smart, strong, and loving women in my life. My mother, my aunts, my sisters, a few girlfriends along the trail. But one shines brighter than all others, and she has been a beacon of inspiration and support for me throughout these past six years. Her name is Tamika.

I had just started my first year of full-time teaching at Laurel High and felt like I had finally gotten my sea legs after two months. I didn't know it yet, but Tamika had recently started student teaching in a separate building at the high school. She was in the academic area, and I was teaching in the vocational wing. Tamika had graduated from the University of Southern Mississippi a couple years earlier, but she went back for a year to get a degree in education and just needed to complete her student teaching to receive her certificate. I started hearing whisperings about Tamika shortly after she arrived, and some of the students began joking with me about her.

"Mr. Owens, you gotta meet Miss Chandler," said one of the girls in my class. "You would really like her, and I'll bet she'd like to go out with you. You have to show some initiative, Mr. Owens, like you always say in class."

"Now, Pam, you need to worry a little more about learning computers and a little less about who I'm dating," I replied, and I tried to change the topic. This was not something I wanted to discuss with students. This conversation went on with various students almost every day for over a week, however, until I finally decided I had better find out who this Tamika was and meet her personally.

It turns out that Tamika and I had many students in common, and they were telling her the same thing. "Miss Chandler, Mr. Owens is a hunk. But he's a little slow, and you may have to make the first move. You can't teach here and not go out with him at least once," her students said. "It wouldn't be natural." Of course, Tamika was involved with somebody else at the time—as was I. Neither of us had much initial interest in the other, and we were both more concerned about school than each other. Still, we had to meet.

One day, Tamika stayed late with one of her students in the library and had to walk her to my class so she wouldn't get in trouble for wandering the hallways during school hours.

"Mr. Owens, I kept Virginia late in class today," she told me when they arrived. "Sorry about that, but I wanted you to know she was with me and shouldn't be reprimanded."

"That's fine, Ms. Chandler," I said. "No worries."

Hardly an exciting introduction, but at least we had finally met. Virginia confessed months later that she and some friends had arranged for her to stay late in class that day so Tamika would have to walk her to my class. They were a cabal of matchmakers.

One of the teachers at the school knew both of us quite well, and she had actually been one of Tamika's teachers when she attended school at Northeast Jones High School in Laurel. She pulled us both aside separately, saying that we should give it a chance. She knew that we were going out with other people at the time, but she also knew neither of our relationships was serious. She thought we would be great together, and she wasn't reluctant to let us know. It seemed like everybody was colluding to make this happen. We just nodded politely and went about our business. We both wanted to focus on learning our new profession, and neither of us was interested in starting a relationship.

During her two months of student teaching, Tamika and I would bump into each other periodically at school events or staff meetings. Since I was just starting out as a teacher, she wanted to hear my perspective on things. I had also developed a website to help student teachers and new teachers get acclimated, and I put a lot of lesson plans, personal thoughts, and various documents online that might be helpful. When her student teaching was finally finished, I told Tamika to email me if she had any questions or if I could help in any way. It was the polite thing to do, and I thought that was the end of that. It wasn't.

Tamika was to graduate in December from the University of Southern Mississippi, the same school I had attended. After completing her student teaching, she had been immediately certified. While waiting for formal graduation, she learned of a full-time opening at Prentiss Middle School, about sixty miles away. She applied for the job and got it immediately. This was a school in a lower income area with high teacher turnover, and it had many troubled kids. The school administration was happy to get Tamika onboard, and she started working full time.

Shortly after starting at Prentiss, Tamika emailed me with a question about some information on my website. I called her back, and we started talking through some teaching and administrative matters at Prentiss. She asked about the students at Laurel High and told me that she had loved student teaching there. Soon we were chatting regularly. We went to a play together, and I attended her teachers' banquet in the spring. We were just friends working our way through a new profession at the time, but something was beginning to click. We would often talk about how the kids and even some faculty members at Laurel High kept trying to get us together, and it never failed to bring a laugh. It seemed to have worked.

Neither of us was anxious to get involved in a serious way because we had both recently broken up with the people we were dating. We kept talking, however, and one day when I was visiting her, we stopped at the local Walmart to pick up some items for her apartment. We turned the corner in an aisle and bumped into several students we had together at Laurel High. Of course, they immediately started laughing and teasing us.

"I knew it, I knew it, I knew it!" one of them exclaimed.

"Mr. Owens, we told you to go out with Miss Tamika. I didn't think you had it in you, but you're a hound dog," said another.

"Miss Tamika, why didn't you tell us? We deserve an agent's fee for this, you know. You would have had to pay Match.com, so pay up."

It was all very humorous, and they made a big deal of it—as if they had solved a mystery and accomplished a great feat.

Shortly afterwards, Tamika and I went to the Bay Fest Fair, which is a big annual event in Bay Springs, Mississippi. I enjoy doing daredevil type things and sought out the fastest rides with the most abrupt twists and turns I could find. Tamika tolerated this—probably because it was early in the relationship—but it was not her first choice. We had a great time together all the same, and I spent countless dollars trying to win her a teddy bear at several of the booths. I didn't succeed, and Tamika joked, "You're spending so much on this, they'll probably give you a real bear before you're done."

As we were walking along, our hands met by accident. At least I think it was by accident. We walked around holding hands for the rest of our visit at the festival, and we shared our first goodnight kiss later that evening.

This was hardly high drama, but we both sensed that this might be going somewhere farther than either of us initially expected.

As the new school year approached, I was spending most of my afternoons coaching football and preparing for the next year at Collins Middle School. Tamika had decided not to teach at Prentiss, which was well over an hour away, and got a position at Laurel Alternative School nearby. This was a school that worked with troubled kids, many of whom came from broken homes, who had been expelled permanently from their regular schools. Before getting her teacher's license, Tamika had worked for a year in this type of environment, and she was a natural for the job. This was her first full-time teaching position. We were both excited about the upcoming year, and we were studying together to get supplemental teaching endorsements before the new school year started. On August 5, 2005, I was supposed to meet up with Tamika after getting the car with Cedrick and Voncarie. But I never made it to our appointment. The accident happened before I even made it to Hattiesburg to meet my brothers…things changed forever.

Tamika had been a bit annoyed that I hadn't shown up or called her that evening, but she sensed something was wrong. She knew it wasn't like me to not show up, and she decided to withhold judgment until she learned more. She was dozing around midnight when she got a call from Cedrick. She was shocked to learn of the day's events. She stayed up the rest of the night and was there at Forrest General before 6 a.m. the next morning, waiting to see me in the ICU.

When I say I had many visitors at Forrest General and later at the Methodist Rehab Center in Jackson, Tamika and my Mom are always the first to come to mind. Visiting hours in the ICU were limited to one morning and one afternoon session, and Tamika was there every day. I was in a stupor throughout much of that time, but she came anyway. She and my mom spent so much time together during that period that they began to form a fast friendship. They sat by my side; they prayed together for my recovery; and they encouraged me and each other along the way. When I was finally moved from the ICU to a regular hospital room, Tamika continued to visit every day and spent every weekend there as well.

Throughout most of my time at Forrest General, I was in extreme pain and moving from one surgery to the next. My thinking was often clouded, and I looked at the world through a haze caused by the many medications I was taking. I substituted intuition for hard thinking, and I felt things more than I thought about them. Tamika's presence was always calming and reassuring. It was comforting and loving. It was uplifting and encouraging. What I didn't understand was why she would do all this, knowing that my very survival was in question and that at best, my future was bleak.

But stay she did, and while many friends came and went, she was there to greet them, give them updates and encouragement about my condition, and help the family keep things together. Mom was there almost every minute of every day, and she would never leave unless Tamika was there to stand in for her. She would only entrust me to Tamika, and we all developed a powerful bond that goes beyond the powers of explanation.

That period of time was tough for Tamika on many levels. She was in her first year of full-time teaching and had many commitments at school. She was distracted because of me, however, and even though she was successful and popular at school, her heart wasn't always in it. No matter what, she tried to make it to the hospital and visit virtually every evening. I came to depend on her presence even though I wasn't very communicative about it, and I felt out of sorts on those rare occasions when she couldn't be there. As I look back on it now, I realize that I was beginning to fall in love with Tamika even though I had no idea at the time.

"Hey, Dwight. How you doin' today? I know. Another day in paradise," Tamika joked.

I was as positive in spirit as I could be at Forrest General, but no day was an easy day, and Tamika knew it. She just took whatever came in stride, dealt with me as she found me, and was always a calming, steady presence. She never treated me like an invalid or a person who should feel sorry for himself. She is the eternal realist and always said, "Dwight, this is gonna be a long, hard road. But you're a strong man with the character to match it. I believe in you." It was hard to be despondent when dealing with a spirit like hers every day.

It was a big change when I finally relocated to the Methodist Rehabilitation Center in Jackson. Because it was about ninety miles away, Tamika couldn't visit every day. She made up for it on weekends, however, and she would arrive after work on Friday, spend Friday and Saturday nights there, and go back home on Sunday. She would also call during the week just to let me know she was thinking about me, and she would tell me about her school day. She watched me in rehab and praised my progress. She met my new friends and joked around with Ryan; she brought me notes and well wishes from friends at school and in town; and she was my lifeline to the outside world. We talked; we watched movies; we watched sports, (not her favorite thing); and sometimes we would actually leave the center. I would roll down to her car, and she would drive to various places in Jackson. The rehab staff was training her as well as me, and she had learned how to take the wheels off my wheelchair so it would fit in the trunk of her car. This took less than a minute to do after she got used to it, and she would say with a grin, "I want to enter a speed competition for this. I'm getting really good at it."

It was great to get out, but I still felt uncomfortable about being seen in public. I didn't like people staring at me. I didn't like the pity. And I didn't like leaving an environment I was comfortable with to face challenges I didn't feel quite ready for. I loved being with her all the same, and I loved riding around and having a sense of freedom and mobility. I knew one of the first things I would do when I got out of rehab would be to get my driver's license upgraded so I'd be able to move around on my own.

Tamika's birthday was coming up in September, and I thought it was about time I did a little something for her to show my gratitude and affection. I had been struggling mightily with our relationship because I couldn't believe in my heart that she could actually want to be with me. Since I had been in rehab, I had seen wives leave husbands, husbands leave wives, and families abandon their disabled family members. It was heartbreaking, and the effects could be devastating. I didn't want to get my heart broken or break hers, and I felt she could have a better and more normal life with somebody else. Tamika was beyond a true and loyal friend, but could we really build a loving relationship? I didn't think so, and I kept trying to push her away even though my efforts were only half-hearted. In addition, most of my energy and thoughts had to be focused on me. It wasn't that I was selfish, but I had to work to get stronger, learn to do things independently, push myself beyond my own personal expectations, and face my limitations all at the same time. I did this every day, and I worked with other people in similar situations to help them as best I could. I didn't feel capable of accepting her affection as anything more than an ironclad bond of friendship.

From her perspective, things were simply what they were. Her highs were never too high, her lows never too low, and her spirits never wavered. Tamika was always realistic, but she was also optimistic and big hearted about everything.

Before Tamika arrived on the weekend of her birthday, I rolled down to the gift shop at rehab to see what I could get for her. Most of the items were intended for patients and not visitors, so the selection was limited. I did what I could, however, and purchased some balloons to celebrate the day, some notepads that happened to have her initial "T" on them, and other knick-knacks I could find. I had also arranged with the cafeteria to prepare a special meal for her. I made sure it was hot and ready to eat when she arrived. It wasn't much, but it was at least an acknowledgment.

When Tamika arrived, I met her with a big smile, a hug, and a bunch of blown-up balloons. I gave her the small gifts I had gathered, and I told her I loved her and was grateful for her help and friendship. Tamika, to this point always a rock and in full control of her emotions, couldn't contain herself. She broke down in tears and started sobbing at the gifts.

"Damn, Tamika," I joked. "If I had known balloons had that effect on you, I would have gotten you some long ago."

She tried to speak and laugh between the tears, but she was overwhelmed by the gesture. "Dwight, thank you," she said in between sobs and sniffles. "With everything you're going through, I just can't believe you thought to do this for me. It's the best birthday ever."

Later that weekend we went for a drive, and I confessed my love for her. I also told her that her big heart shouldn't cloud her sharp mind. I didn't expect anything more than what we had, and I was just grateful to have her in my life. This brought more tears, and she said that she had loved me all along. She wasn't going anywhere. It was the most wonderful weekend of my life.

There is great depth in Tamika. She is my friend. She is my hero. And now she is my wife.

8

A GLORIOUS HOMECOMING

I t was the end of October in 2005, and it was time to leave rehab. I had mixed feelings about it. I had been there for two months, much longer than any other patient, and I was the new "vet." I knew everybody there, welcomed all the new arrivals, and made myself helpful by counseling patients at various stages of their rehab. I mattered, and I was doing something to help other people. I had made a promise to God that if I got through this thing, I would dedicate myself to helping others in a similar situation, and I was trying to make good on that promise. Even though I still had a long way to go, I was farther down the road than others, and I could imagine them thinking, "Well, if he can do it, so can I." I really didn't want to face a new set of challenges, but I knew it had to happen. I was as ready as I was ever going to be, and it was time to leave.

The day I left, we had a "double floor" pizza party—a boatload of pizzas for everybody on the rehab floor and on the nursing floor, where my room was. We dined in fine style during my final rehab session at the center and throughout the afternoon. I said all my goodbyes, received more hugs and kisses than I'd ever gotten in my life, and wiped more than a few tears from my own cheeks and from others'. I received gift baskets and a St. Louis cap and t-shirt from one of the nurses, and I had a long chat with the staff psychiatrist who had worked closely with me throughout my time there. She thanked me for making her job easy and, more importantly, for helping her with the other patients. The whole day was uplifting and helped steady my nerves for the next chapter in my life.

Mom and a few friends were there on my last day to help check me out of the facility and make sure I was set to go. I rolled down to the transport van, got inside, and started the trek home. I exchanged a brief greeting with the driver, and we got underway. The trip was about ninety minutes. I was the only passenger in the van because Mom and my friends had to drive their own cars back, so I had time for reflection. I was proud of the work I had done in rehab. Although my body was battered when I'd arrived, I'd found a way to get through it all. I still had many medical problems and would need a lot of home health care, but I was getting better. I also knew it had been a team effort, and I had the best support group the world could provide. I had a loving family, friends who wouldn't let me down, a rehab staff that was spectacular in every way, and a reverend who raised my spirits. Most importantly, I felt I had God in my corner. I had spent many hours praying and having internal conversations with God during those past two months, and I found solace and strength in the relationship. As Mom often said, "Dwight, a path will unfold before you. You just have to be ready to accept it." I began to believe she was right, and I was filled with gratitude in my heart and a renewed love of life as we wound our way home.

I was lost in my thoughts for most of the trip home, and I was caught off guard when the van turned onto the road leading to my house. There were balloons on several mailboxes, and I remember thinking how odd that was. Had somebody had a child and nobody told me? The mystery was solved moments later when we pulled into the driveway and I saw balloons all over the place, a huge "Welcome Home, Dwight" banner on the front of the house, and a large gathering of people cheering my return.

I had been surprised and perhaps a bit disappointed that so few people had come to visit me during my last weekend at rehab, and now the reason was clear. Many of them had been busy preparing for my arrival and planning a welcome home party. Mom and Tamika had been preparing the house, getting the food together, and arranging for many friends to be there. I had to take a minute before I could get out of the van and dry my eyes. I'm something of a crybaby at times like this, and I had to gather myself. But I wasn't all that successful—the tears came right back when everybody started clapping and cheering as I rolled out of the van.

It was a blissful moment that brings me a smile to this day. Everybody was happy to be there, happy to greet me, and happy that I had advanced to a new phase. Surrounded by people I loved and receiving countless hugs and handshakes, I was thrilled to be home. It was a delight to see everybody, get caught up, and just feel the high spirits all around me. Although Tamika couldn't be there because of a family matter, she had still helped Mom to prepare. Both of them had put in a lot of work, as they do with everything, and I was beaming to see my mother laughing and smiling. And…I finally got to greet a very important friend.

During my whole time at rehab there was one family member I missed terribly, and he had never once come to visit. His name was Rocky, and he was our pet Chihuahua. An impressive four pounds of energy and attitude, I loved the little guy. When I finally made my way into the house, Rocky took one look, sped toward my chair as fast as his tiny legs could carry him, and leapt into my lap. I couldn't keep him off me for the next hour, and each time I tried, he leapt back up in a matter of seconds. The feeling was mutual. Over the next few weeks, Rocky never left my side. He slept under my wheelchair, and I almost ran over him more than a few times. What Rocky lacked in size, he more than made up for in heart.

The party lasted a couple of hours, and it was a glorious homecoming. I felt the strength and love of the community in my heart. It had to come to an end, however, and when it did, I just basked in the glow of the moment. I was home again, and it felt like I had closed another arc on the circle of my life. Everything felt right.

9

LEARNING THE NEW NORMAL

There was a lot to absorb as I awoke the next morning. I was startled when I first opened my eyes and realized there were no nurses chatting in the hallway. I was not lying in a hospital bed. There would be no breathing exercises or rehab to start the day. It took a few moments for the realization to sink in: things were different, yet in many ways the same. I still had a long way to go in my recovery, and I would have home health care for the next several months. Now, however, it was mostly on me. I had to take charge and do rehab largely on my own. I had to stand tall and start dealing with the world around me, and that would be the toughest thing of all. My homecoming party was wonderful but short-lived, and now I had to press on and earn my independence. I had to learn a new normal, and I had to sort through a mix of emotions—anxiety, fear, but most of all, determination. I had gotten this far and had to keep going no matter what.

Our home had been extensively modified in my absence. Mom had put a great deal of thought and time into completing the renovations, and she did it all while still visiting me every weekend during rehab. I recognized that this was just one more reason to admire and love her, and I was grateful. I yearned to be fully self-reliant, but I knew I couldn't get there without the help she provided every day.

There was a ramp leading up to the front door so I could get in and out on my own. All the doors had been replaced and the doorways, which had been the standard twenty-eight inches wide, were expanded to thirty-six inches so that my wheelchair could pass through. The doors now opened away from me because it's quite difficult to sit in a wheelchair, pull a door toward you, and then maneuver around it and through the doorway. All the handles now had levers instead of knobs, which made them much easier to open. Furniture was rearranged so I could move around without banging into everything…which I still managed to do anyway. A wonderful organization in Mississippi called Vocational Rehab had provided all the renovations free of charge. I could not live in a home without these modifications, and they graciously paid the bill. But on her own, Mom had paid to have a spacious room added to the side of the house for me to use as my rehab area.

CW, a friend of the family who had expert carpentry skills, had contributed his considerable abilities to helping get the house ready for my arrival. He knew something about everything when it came to building, and he took this work personally. CW's work was meticulous, and he thought everything through before he did it. He would often say to his son, who worked with him, "It's always better to measure twice and cut once. You may think it takes longer to be cautious, but you save money and time in the long run." He wanted to get it right the first time.

In addition to the many other renovations, CW had built a large balcony off the back of the house so I could relax there, enjoy the sunset, and just think. He also built a ramp off the back so I could get in and out from there. In the coming weeks, I would often sit there and watch the cars drive by on the highway. The travelers got used to seeing me, and many were people I already knew. They would wave and honk their horns whenever they saw me, and sometimes they rolled down their windows and yelled, "Hey, Dwight, lookin' good!" Tamika would often join me there late in the afternoon, and people just seemed to enjoy seeing us together. In a way, I had become like a landmark for the community, and they were all invested in my recovery.

Rehab really only begins at the rehab center and then continues for the rest of your life. I had learned a great deal at the center, and perhaps the most important thing was to keep up with an exercise and rehab regimen. Many people become despondent and lethargic after leaving the strict schedule and positive surroundings at rehab, and they stop exercising. They lose the benefits of all the good work they did to get through it in the first place, and they take a giant step backwards. I had made a deal with God, and I wouldn't let that happen to me. That promise, however, proved easier to make than to keep.

I still had a lot of healing to do, and doctors, nurses, and therapists came by every day except Sunday. I felt like I had my own personal MASH unit at home. They poked and prodded; took blood; checked my breathing, temperature, and blood pressure; made sure I hadn't caught any infections; looked for bruising and massaged my legs; and tried to keep me on the right path. I came to love these people for all they did to help me and for their willing, giving spirits.

The therapists came at least every other day, and they sometimes worked as a team. They taught me how to get plates out of cabinets without dropping them, how to nudge the cereal box off the top shelf so it would fall into my lap where I could catch it, how to transfer to my bed or couch; how to deal with slopes or ramps when in a wheelchair, and much, much more.

One of the more indelicate things a paralyzed person has to deal with is bowel and bladder control. We don't feel the sensations or get the same warning signals we used to. It's one reason many paralyzed people are reluctant to go out in public, but there are ways around it. In my case, I trained my body over the course of about six months by going to the bathroom at specific times during the day, whether I needed to or not. As the months passed, my body learned my schedule, and it began to adapt to it. I always have to be sensitive to what time it is, and I can never disengage my mind or get fully lost in the moment. That could result in an embarrassing scene for everybody. It's just the way it is. Many people in wheelchairs also use disposable catheter bags, which they can hide. But I find them a big nuisance and don't use them. I prefer my system, and I stick to my precise schedule to avoid any problems.

Therapy at home was as grueling as at the rehab center, and there was no escape. The physical therapist worked hard to make my body stronger and more flexible by having me exercise and practice stretching techniques every day. I learned how to stretch myself as far as possible, until I was even able to put my own socks on while sitting in the wheelchair. This was a really big deal because it required me to stretch and balance at the same time.

"Dwight, this is a whole new reality now," my occupational therapist told me. "Beds are hard to deal with, and we've got to develop some new techniques for transfers."

Transferring on and off a bed was extremely difficult for two reasons. First, the bed was not at the same height as the wheelchair, so I had to lift myself to a higher level as I shifted sideways from my chair. To compound the problem, I would sink into the soft mattress. I had to learn to use my hands to place my feet precisely in the correct position to keep my balance, push on a soft surface that seemed to sink down forever, make a strenuous leap using only my arm strength, and land in the middle of the wheelchair. It didn't always work out that way. Sometimes I would miss and hit the sides of the wheelchair or otherwise begin to tumble. It was hard, frustrating, and often painful work, and I felt like I was taking a graduate course in gymnastics. My arms were definitely strong enough for the maneuver, but nobody has ever described me as graceful. We practiced the transfer for hours on end, and the therapists had to catch me time and again as I was about to fall.

"I do believe you have a personal disdain for gravity," the therapist joked. "We need to make gravity your friend, not your mortal enemy."

The therapists weren't there all the time, and I had many near misses along the way. I would forget to lock my wheelchair, and when I pushed off to make the jump to the bed, it would go flying in a different direction. Of course, this would disrupt the maneuver, and I would miss the bed completely. Fortunately, I never did any real damage to myself, and the only thing wounded was my pride. Mom, Tamika, or my stepfather, Eric, would hear the commotion and come running. They would see me on the floor, help haul all 220 pounds of me back into the chair, and often break out in a laugh. It was part of the learning process, and we all took it in stride. It took almost two months of daily practice to perfect the process.

I left the rehab center in late October, and after a few weeks at home I decided to take a rare trip out of the house. I didn't like being in public or being the center of attention among strangers, and I was reluctant to leave the comfortable surroundings of home. Perhaps it's a character flaw that I preferred to stay put and avoid the world outside. But Christmas was around the corner, and on this day, I got up the nerve and asked Tamika to drive me to Lowe's. I wanted to get Mom a couple of things for the house as Christmas gifts.

Tamika and I were going down an aisle when we saw a little girl no older than four tugging on her mother's sleeve.

"Mommy, Mommy. I want one of those for Christmas." Of course, she was pointing at my wheelchair and thought it was the best toy ever.

I just laughed and gave them both a big grin. "Sweetheart, I sure am glad to have this wheelchair, but I don't think you want one," I said.

I could sense the girl's mom sigh in relief, and she smiled back at me. I would have liked to hear the chat they no doubt had later that day. Tamika and I both love the honesty and spontaneity of children, and we had a good laugh about it on the way home.

My closest friend from rehab, Ryan, and I talked often once I got home, and he was doing great. He was attending college, and he had found a way to use his remarkable athletic ability. He had taken up wheelchair fencing, and he was a natural. Fast, agile, and with reflexes like a cat, Ryan quickly caught the attention of the Paralympics fencing coach in Louisville, Kentucky. He had a new love, and it had a sharp point at the end of it.

Ryan called one day to say, "Hey, Coach, how you doin'? Guess what? I won three matches today, and guess where I'm going?" He didn't pause to let me guess before giving the answer. "The coach wants me on the Paralympic team, and we're having a competition in Montreal next week."

Ryan's enthusiasm never waned, and he loved his new sport. He told me he worked at it six hours a day, sometimes more. He is currently ranked first in his particular grouping and twenty-third in the nation overall. It was a stunning rise to the top, and he is on his way to the International Paralympic Games.

I was, in a sense, doing my own athletic training as well. One of the biggest problems with paralysis is poor circulation. There is always a fear of blood clots, which can be life threatening. To prevent clotting, paralyzed people have to find a way to work their legs regularly even though they can't move them on their own. This won't entirely eliminate the risk of blood clots, but it can minimize it. I had a motorized bike put in my rehab room to help work my legs and improve my circulation. My cousin Greg would help place me on the seat and strap my feet into the pedals, and I would then exercise my legs for thirty minutes or so at a time. Of course, I couldn't use my legs to pedal—which is why the bike had to be motorized.

In addition to improving blood flow and reducing the risk of clotting, this exercise also helped prevent my legs from atrophying and minimized urinary tract infections. UTIs tend to plague people in wheelchairs because we have to sit in the same place all the time, and they can only be prevented by walking and other physical activity that most people do during the normal course of a day.

So, to me, my bike was a big help in a number of ways. It never occurred to me that it also presented a danger. One unhappy day in February of 2006, I was pedaling away and lost in another world. I was listening to my headphones and didn't realize that my left foot had come loose from its straps. I was pedaling on and on, and with each stroke the pedal hit my ankle or the bottom of my foot. When I finally noticed what had happened, I yelled out to Greg, who came running to help. The banging of the pedal caused severe swelling and bruising. It was a grim reminder that I simply had to pay better attention.

When the swelling did not go down, we realized that I would have to visit my old home away from home, Forrest General Hospital. I loved the people there, but I wasn't happy to become a part of their lives again. I still had a pick line attached to me so doctors and nurses could inject me more easily, and I was immediately placed on IV antibiotics. I had to stay in bed for two weeks in the hospital, which is the most boring thing in the world. The doctor finally sent me home, but my foot still wasn't healing, so of course the prescription was more bed rest. All I did was move from a hospital bed to my own bedroom.

To pass the time, I would sit up as best I could and lift weights for hours. Once I burned out, I would rest for an hour and do it again. I was angry and frustrated, and I felt like God was just piling it on. Hadn't he made his point already? It seemed like every time I made a small advance, there would be a setback to match it. It wasn't fair, and I spent more time feeling sorry for myself than I did trying to work through the problem. Tamika and Mom would try to lift my spirits, cook special meals for me, and be as positive as possible to help me through this latest problem, but I was stubbornly frustrated and despondent. I'm not proud of it.

After another two weeks at home, there was no visible sign of healing, and the skin on my foot was discolored and decaying. I decided to call my old friend Dr. Donald, the trauma surgeon who had done so much for me along the way.

"There may be a better solution, Dwight," he said. "The wound isn't healing properly, and I think a skin graft may serve you better." At this point I was so anxious to recover and get out of bed, I would have been willing to put leeches on the sore if it was what he suggested. I would try anything that offered some promise of improvement. Dr. Donald completed the skin graft and sent me back home on more bed rest. I had come to hate those words—I thought I was the most rested person in the world. But the operation was successful and the wound healed within a week.

Even though I had to stay in bed for weeks and could not move my left leg, the physical and occupational therapists kept showing up during that entire period of time. They did what they could with me. We were very limited, but we did devise one ingenious exercise. I was having pain and problems with my shoulder from the rotator cuff surgery, and I needed to stretch and exercise my arm. We decided to attach a rope and pulley to my bedroom door. I could pull on the rope with my right hand and that would lift and stretch my left arm. It hurt terribly, but pain meant progress. I would do this repeatedly throughout the day until tears formed and I couldn't take it anymore.

Again and again, I thought back to my Dad's exhortations when I was a kid. "Tough it out, Dwight. You can deal with the pain. It's part of life," he would say. Like me, he was a big crybaby when it came to things that touched the heart, but he was made of stone when the issue was physical.

Tamika visited almost every day, and she was a great help, especially when it came to dealing with doctors and the hospital. Tamika would ask the doctors questions I should have thought of and double check to make sure she understood what they wanted me to do. She made it her business to keep me on track. I felt like she was my personal agent, and I knew she would follow up with calls to the doctor's office if anything seemed off or if we needed additional information. She would drive me to my medical appointments every week and often several times a week, and she would be with me in the examination room when I met with the doctor. Over time, the doctors came to trust her more than they trusted me, and sometimes it felt like I didn't really need to be there at all as long as she was.

Even the physical and occupational therapists began to work with Tamika and my mother. "Now, Tamika, you have to lift his legs like this to help his circulation. Dwight can't feel it when he's got too much weight pressing on the plates of the wheelchair, and you need to make sure he moves them frequently. This helps prevent blistering and sores," the physical therapist would explain to her. The occupational therapist in turn would show Tamika and my mom how to arrange things in the refrigerator so I could reach them easily. Sometimes it seemed like they spent more time teaching them how to take care of me than they did making sure I could take care of myself. Tamika and Mom were eager students and a wonderful blessing, although it took them a long time to understand that I could do a great many things on my own, and that's the way I wanted it. A few times when they were overly helpful, I had to remind them to let me do things on my own even though it took me a long time. It just pained them to watch me struggle, so they were always at the ready with a helping hand.

Most days passed slowly at home, and the others passed slower yet. Everybody else was at work during the day, and although Greg and Mom would swing by early every morning, I was mostly on my own until Tamika showed up late in the afternoon. Rocky was my early warning system for her arrival; he seemed to recognize the sound of her car a mile away. He would run to the front of the house, give a few barks, and start pawing at the door. Once this ritual started, I knew Tamika would poke her head through in about two minutes. This was always the happiest moment of my day, and I would get antsy and a little grumpy whenever she had to stay late at work.

"Hey, Dwight, what's kickin'?" she would ask and give me a smile. Then she'd sit on the side of the bed and recount the day's events. I didn't have many events to recount, which annoyed me, so we mostly talked about her day. What happened at school, which kids were driving her crazy, and what the teaching staff was up to. It gave me something good to think about and something to look forward to each day. I still refused to think of us as a couple exactly, but I don't know what I would have done without her. Every once in a while I would test the waters and let her know she didn't have to do all this.

"Now, hush Dwight. You're just being goofy. I'm not going anywhere, so get used to it," she would laugh and change the topic. With my many physical setbacks and permanent paralysis, I still couldn't trust it all, even though I realized she was the steadiest, most reliable person I had ever known in my life.

Not every day was boring, and there were two in particular that made my heart beat just a little bit faster. One day, quite unexpectedly, I received a large package in the mail. It was a bundle of about fifty letters from students I had taught during my days at Collins Middle High School and from the football players I had coached at Laurel High. Collins Middle School Superintendent Ike Sanford had asked the students who knew me to send me letters, and they took their work seriously. The letters were joyous. There were expressions of sympathy about the accident, exhortations to keep my spirits up, and many, many personal touches. Some kids wrote stories of things that had happened in class, talked about the math they were studying, and even joked about their conspiracy to get Tamika and me together. I had connected in a special way with many of these kids, and I could see each of their faces in my mind's eye. Their letters were far more than an assignment. They were heartfelt for the students and heartwarming for me. I still read them on occasion, and I am always moved.

About a month later, in April of 2006, I received a call from Mr. Sanford asking if he could come by for a visit. He had a couple of things he wanted to discuss, and he left it at that. We arranged to meet the next day, and I was filled with anticipation. I didn't know what he had in mind, but I sensed it was a good thing.

"Hi, Dwight," he said with a bright smile. "I've been planning to meet with you for a while, but I heard about your foot problem and wanted to give you some time."

"It's great to see you, Mr. Sanford. I really miss the kids and the football team. I wish I was there."

"Well, in part that's what I wanted to talk about. The kids, I mean," Mr. Sanford said, "But first things first. You've been receiving a check from the school district since your accident, and I want you to know that the teachers in the district have donated another two hundred sick days to you. That means you'll continue to have an income for at least another year, and you'll probably receive more days in the months ahead. I wanted to assuage any concerns you might have in that regard. Everybody admires the courage and determination you've shown throughout this ordeal, and the teachers came to me with this suggestion. You've touched many lives."

I was stunned by this information and overwhelmed with gratitude. I didn't cry, which was an accomplishment of sorts, but I came close. I had only taught for one full year and part of a second, and I had never even met many of the teachers who donated their sick days to me. It was a touching act of generosity, and it made me feel embarrassed that I had ever felt sorry for myself.

"But that's not what I really came to talk about," said Mr. Sanford. "I think you need a goal and something to work toward. I want to talk with you about becoming a public speaker and sharing your story with a broad audience, with schoolkids in particular," he went on. "You're a charismatic guy, a person the kids can relate to. More importantly, you have a cautionary tale that can have real impact. You can save lives. I'd like you to think about this, and then we can chat some more when you're ready. In the meantime, I brought you some DVDs and other material about inspirational speakers. I think you'll find them interesting. When you're ready, I can arrange for you to speak at schools in our district, and I think we might be able to compensate you as well. I also know most of the other superintendents in the state, and I'm sure they would love to have you speak at their schools. It's a chance to turn your personal tragedy into a triumph, and I know you would be terrific at it. We're on your side."

I was dumbfounded and not sure how to respond. I had been approached already by the Mississippi Department of Transportation and done some work on drunk driving and seatbelt safety for them, but I hadn't been the primary speaker before a large group. I had been asked to speak on several occasions, but my recovery had been so slow with so many setbacks that I had to turn those requests down. I told Mr. Sanford how grateful I was to the teachers and asked him to let them know. I told him how much I appreciated his visit and that I would study the materials he gave me. I would get back to him soon.

I'll confess that with the pain I was still suffering, the foot setback that put me in bed for almost six weeks, and a general sense of malaise, I had let my spirits fall. Mr. Sanford's visit was just the thing I needed at just the right time. His visit, the generous donation from the teachers, and the letters from the students made my spirits soar. I knew I had to take charge and honor their faith in me. I would accomplish nothing by feeling sorry for myself. I had to get moving and take responsibility for my own attitude and recovery.

I also knew that I had not kept up my agreement with God to help other people in my situation, and I wanted to get back on track. I had been a reliable churchgoer all my life, but I had avoided it the past few months. It was time for a change. I spoke with my preacher, Reverend Evans, and he asked me to speak before the church in a couple of weeks. I wanted to address the youth group in particular and share something of my story with them.

I felt a mix of queasiness and anticipation as I got ready to address the congregation. This was my home turf. I knew everybody, and they all knew my story, but I still felt a sense of unease before speaking. They had supported me during the past ten months with visits, cards, prayers, and weekly updates at church. Many had been at my homecoming party. They had held fundraisers to help pay some of my medical bills, and they had been with me every step of the way. I had thanked Reverend Evans many times, but I had never thanked the congregation personally. This was my chance. I wanted them to know how much their love and support had sustained me. I wanted them to know they made a difference, and I was grateful beyond my ability to express it. I wanted to make the most of this opportunity.

The church was completely silent as I rolled down the center aisle to speak. Everybody looked at me with an eager interest and a genuine desire to hear what I had to say. I saw love and respect in their faces, and there was kindness in their eyes. It was a bit awkward at first, but they leaned into every word as I talked about the accident, about Forrest General, about my days in rehab, and about my recent setbacks. They wanted to know how I felt about Herman Posey, and I explained that I had forgiven and stopped thinking about him months ago. I had no interest in revenge, and he wasn't my problem. My problem was to keep my spirits and my recovery on track.

A whisper of "Amen" went through the congregation when I talked about Posey and about forgiveness. Our job isn't to exact revenge, it's to move on and do the best we can, be the best people we can be. I talked about my mother's faith and her relentless preaching to me, and I jokingly suggested she stand in for the reverend the next time he went on vacation. I talked about Tamika and her strength of character. By the time I was done, there were tears in the eyes of the parishioners, and I received a standing ovation. I felt I didn't deserve it. I had been less than the man I thought I should be on far too many occasions. They understood and accepted my failings, and they made me beam with happiness. I was at home among my church family, and the whole thing was one big loving embrace.

It also made me feel like I was finally ready to make a contribution to the world again. I was ready to honor my promise to God.

I received a similar response from the youth group later that morning, and I was moved by their concern and affection. About a hundred members were there, ranging from early school-age children to young adults attending college. They asked questions of every sort, and the young children were particularly enthusiastic.

"Does your mama have to move your legs every day, Mr. Dwight?" one girl asked.

"When are you gonna start walking again?" asked another.

"How do you go to the bathroom?" asked a third.

It still makes me laugh to think of how open they were with their questions, and how eager they were to learn everything. I spoke for well over an hour, and by the time we were done, I knew that I wanted to do it again and again. I was ready to get started.

I was ready, but my body wasn't quite with the program yet. I woke up one morning shortly after my presentation at church, and I was suffocating. I could barely manage even a partial breath, and I thought I had reached the end.

I remember thinking, "Maybe God just wanted me to regain my spirit before he was done with me." I thought these were probably the last few moments of my life, and I was okay with that. My wonderful dream and the visions I experienced when I coded shortly after the accident were never far from my mind, and I no longer had any fear of dying. I'm in no rush to get there, but I'll be at ease when the day arrives.

Greg rushed me to the hospital, and they immediately put me on breathing support. It was quickly apparent that I had two problems. My liver had gone on another journey and needed to be put back in its proper place. The thing seemed to have a mind of its own and just didn't want to stay where it belonged. This was causing a great deal of discomfort and internal confusion, and it had to be corrected at once. I also had a tear in my diaphragm, which had made it almost impossible to breathe. I needed immediate surgery, and they wasted no time.

I had been through it all before, and I just rolled my eyes to the sky. "Enough, already," I thought, and I wondered if it would ever end.

After this latest round of surgeries, I remained in the hospital for another two weeks. I was back on IV antibiotics and IV feeding, and I couldn't eat a decent meal for over a month. My breathing, however, improved immediately. I guess it had to. I was uncomfortable and in great pain, but the improvement was instantaneous. I had to begin a new round of breathing exercises again, but they weren't nearly as difficult as they had been before. I also had to turn over every two hours and learn how to sleep in an exact position that minimized the pain. There is nothing comfortable about being in a hospital.

After spending two weeks in the hospital bed, I once again heard those dreaded words: "bed rest." I hated it, but I knew there was no way around it. I was confined to my bed at home for another three weeks. This time, however, I didn't mope or waste time feeling sorry for myself. I was done with that. I would not let this latest misadventure get me down, and I would be true to my resolution to be a positive contributor to the world. I wanted to get better so that I could act on Mr. Sanford's suggestion. I wanted to share my story.

During the next few weeks, I watched every video I could get my hands on about public speaking; I read all the books Tamika would bring me on the topic; and I wrote poems and notes about my experience. I even practiced parts of presentations out loud when I was home alone. There was one more thing, however, that I had to do before launching a career in inspirational speaking.

I contacted the rehab center in Jackson and made arrangements to return after the bed rest was over and I had regained my strength. I needed help with breathing and more work on perfecting my balance and transfers. Most importantly, I needed to become an expert at transferring into the driver's seat of a car and putting my wheelchair in alongside me. I couldn't get my new driver's license without this skill, and it was eating at me that I was still stuck at home relying on other people to drive me everywhere.

The rehab staff welcomed me back and seemed truly glad to see me. It was a fun reunion.

"Dwight, you look great," said Nurse Mary. "You've gained some weight. I never knew you were so handsome!"

My facial scars had finally healed; my arm was greatly improved; and I was anxious to get to work. I was ready to put heart and soul into it.

I went back to rehab for two weeks in August of 2006, and I pushed myself to the limit. I worked with the various therapists to perfect every kind of transfer I might come across, and I worked constantly on "The Car." The rehab center had a full-sized car on the second floor, and I practiced for hours getting myself in and out. I practiced to make sure the wheelchair was in just the right place so I could reach it once I was in the seat, break it down properly, and pull it in alongside me. I was tired of being reluctant to go out in public and tired of looking helpless, and that was going to change. I wanted to go out on my own, and that could only happen if I got my driver's certification.

Tamika visited me on both weekends at rehab and a few times during the week. We went out to dinners and movies, we spent time in parks and window-shopping in the city, and we had a ball together. It took time, but I got used to the stares, and I learned just to smile back at people. They didn't mean any harm, and I realized it was part of my job to make them comfortable with me. Most people were very friendly and helpful, and they would go out of their way to open doors or pick something up if I dropped it. I usually told them that I could do it on my own, and I sometimes explained how important this sense of self-reliance is to people with disabilities.

During this time I also came to realize that I could help able-bodied people deal with people who have disabilities. I could help them get past their discomfort by helping them understand that we are as intellectually capable and generally as independent as they are. I started thinking of many things people do without realizing they are being rude or making matters worse instead of better. I started developing a list that I could make part of my public speaking program.

"Stop staring," for example. "No, really. I can cut my own food all by myself," for another. "No, you really don't have to push my wheelchair. I'm pretty good at getting around by myself," for a third. And many, many others.

I started thinking about how hard it had been for my family not to overdo it and make me feel helpless. They had big hearts but didn't understand in the beginning that I wanted to do everything I could on my own, even if it was harder for me than it would have been for them to just do it. I came up with specific examples of situations I had come across, and I tried to present them in a humorous and positive light.

I fed off the enthusiasm of the rehab staff. I met with the staff psychiatrist who picked up where she had left off the last time we met, and she asked me to meet with new arrivals and to speak with people at various stages of rehab. I had been through home rehab, suffered numerous physical setbacks, been out in public, and faced most of the things they would encounter when they got out. I had a group of people around me throughout my second stay in rehab, and they were all eager to learn something about their future life from somebody who was actually living their reality. Since I was in a wheelchair, my experience carried great weight with the patients, and they wanted to hear from me.

I told them to expect psychological and probably physical setbacks and mood swings that they would have to work through. Nobody could do it for them. Their biggest dangers were complacency and self-pity, and they had to fight those enemies. I told them about all the modifications in my home, how beds were a huge challenge, how it was hard but essential to leave the comfort of their homes, how I had learned to control my bowels and bladder, and how I could do almost everything an able-bodied person could do. Perhaps I couldn't do things as quickly, but I could do them. I told them about organizations that were there to help them, about support groups they might want to join, and about living independently. I told them about Tamika and the love and support of my family and my church. Mostly I told them that they had to take charge. They would be on their own soon, and they had to put the lessons they learned in rehab into practice on the outside.

I didn't realize it until later, but I was actually practicing many of the things I had learned about public speaking. I was getting more and more comfortable with it all the time. When my second rehab stay was over, I realized the other patients had helped me even more than I helped them.

I left rehab for the second time at the end of August with a great attitude and feeling physically the best I had in the past year. I enjoyed a renewed sense of confidence, and I was ready to meet the world head on. It had taken me a long time to get that far, and I was not about to go backwards.

The first thing I did when I got home was call Mississippi State University to arrange for a driver's education course to get my driving certification. They are the only organization that provides this service in the state, and they are experts at what they do. Ryan always talked about how great he felt going from place to place on his own, and he said it was liberating. I wanted that same freedom.

I scheduled a training session for mid-September. In the meantime, Tamika and I got to work looking for a vehicle. We checked out Car-Trader.com, AutoTrader.com, and various Internet sites. We talked about different options and what would be best for me. I knew I didn't want a van because that just shouts, "Disabled person here!" to the world. I wanted a truck or an SUV.

Cedrick drove me to the training facility about two hours away, and we had a great time. It was a road trip with my older brother, and we had been each other's closest friend for all our lives. We teased each other a lot, and at one point after a lull in the conversation, he said, "Dwight, you better pass this damn test. I don't want to drive your sorry ass around for the next fifty years. Plus it will be good for you to get out and do more stuff. Just let me know ahead of time, so I can get off the road first." Cedrick had long ago gotten used to my condition, and he teased me about it periodically.

I responded in kind. "Ugly brother, I'm doing this for my own safety. I don't want to spend the next fifty years in fear of your sloppy driving. I am plenty motivated already."

The training only lasted one day because every student already had their regular driver's license. They just needed to learn the new equipment. After about an hour of lecture time, the instructor put me in a simulator equipped with hand controls for the gas and brakes. It was much like a video game, and the only real issue was making sure I didn't press the accelerator when I meant to hit the brakes. Both functions were on the same control handle on the steering wheel, up for gas and down for brakes, and it all felt quite natural after a couple of hours.

We then went out for a road test on the campus of Mississippi State University, and I was more than a little queasy for the first half hour. I hadn't driven for almost a year, and now my hands were doing what my feet used to do. The driving instructor had his own controls in case something went wrong, but it didn't. I was exceedingly cautious in the beginning but quickly got past any initial discomfort. I did all the things any driver has to do. Parallel parking, K-turns, and backing in and out of parking spots. We went out on the highway and later drove through the city of Jackson. When it was all done at the end of the day, I received my certification and was ready to go. All I needed now was a vehicle with the proper equipment.

The next day, Tamika and I finally made a selection. I bought a Lincoln Navigator over the Internet and arranged for it to be delivered to Hattiesburg the following week. Tamika drove a friend and me there to pick it up, and then she had to drive it back because the vehicle still had to be back-fitted with the proper equipment for me. It sat in my mom's driveway for three weeks before the equipment arrived at Mobility Systems, and all the while I looked at it lovingly and yearned every day to get on the road.

We finally received the call that the equipment had arrived and we could take the car to Hattiesburg to get it installed. We delivered the Navigator the next day. Now I was only a week away from driving…but it felt like the longest week of my life. I was like a kid waiting for Christmas morning, and every minute seemed to pass more and more slowly. Finally, I got the call that my truck was ready. I could come get it any time. It was a great feeling to know I would be on the road on my own soon, and Tamika, Cedrick, and I made the trek back to Hattiesburg the following day. Even though I was brimming with eagerness, I didn't want to be foolish. When I took the certification course, the instructor urged me to spend a day or two on back roads with limited traffic, just to get completely acclimated to the vehicle before driving in cities or heavy traffic. I asked Cedrick to drive the truck home, and I waited until the following morning to go out solo.

I barely slept that night, and when I did, I dreamed about being behind the wheel on my own. The next morning, I rolled down to the truck, got in, and waved goodbye.

"I'll be back. Don't worry about a thing," I said.

I drove off feeling a remarkable sense of freedom. I had come a long way, and I flashed on the most famous line from Martin Luther King's wonderful speech: "Free at last, free at last. Thank God Almighty, I'm free at last." I had completed another step on a long, personal journey. My life was changed for the better, and I was grateful for my increased independence.

I was gone for much of the day. I didn't answer phone calls on my cell phone. I didn't stop to eat. I just drove and drove and drove some more. I started out on back roads but quickly abandoned them for the highway. Of course, the day couldn't pass without at least one glitch, and I got pulled over by a Mississippi Highway Patrolman on my way home. I had been driving too slowly in the left-hand lane, which I found quite humorous. I had never before been at risk of driving too slowly.

The patrolman explained why he had pulled me over, and I told him that I had just gotten the vehicle and was driving it for the first time that day. He saw the hand controls on the steering wheel and immediately understood the issue.

"Mr. Owens, congratulations on getting your vehicle. I have a family member in the same situation, and I know you'll do just fine. Please be especially careful the first couple of days," he suggested, and he gave me a big smile instead of a ticket.

I smiled back, and I felt joy in being alive. Nothing would dampen my spirits on this day. Nothing would slow me down in the days ahead.

10

MAKE IT COUNT FOR SOMETHING

Everybody breathed a sigh of relief when I arrived back home that afternoon, but they were not happy with me.

"Darn it, Dwight. You never answered your phone, and I called five times," Tamika yelled at me. And she was right.

"You had us worried sick," Mom added before Tamika could get in another line.

"That was not right, Dwight. You could have been anywhere. In a ditch. In a hospital. Anything could have happened. You didn't need to make us worry," said Tamika, and it was evident they had tacitly formed a tag team. This went on for a good while, and when one of them began to run out of steam, the other picked up the slack. Greg was amused by the proceedings and smiled broadly at me when Mom and Tamika weren't looking. Otherwise, he put on a serious face and nodded his agreement with whatever they were saying. Greg was enjoying my discomfort because he was usually the one on the receiving end of these conversations. But he was smart enough not to pile on. He knew he would pay a big price later on if he joined the fray.

I had been inconsiderate, and I knew it. Tamika and Mom made sure I knew it, and once they were convinced I'd learned my lesson, they added a few more comments for good measure. I apologized early and often. This, however, had been my first taste of personal freedom in over a year, and I luxuriated in it. I had been out on my own for the first time in ages, and it was liberating. I had travelled half the state of Mississippi and relished each moment. Now that I could drive again, I felt I could face the world on different terms and with a renewed sense of confidence.

Of course, Tamika and Mom forgave me, and they ultimately chose to share in my happiness instead of dissecting my thoughtlessness. Although they nursed their anger for much of the evening, their annoyance started to abate once they understood how much the day had meant to me, how I felt it made me more independent, and how this filled me with pride. I finally understood firsthand why Ryan was so exhilarated when he got his driving certification—how it made him feel "almost" normal.

"This lets me feel self-reliant, less of a burden on everybody," I told Tamika and Mom. "I can go places and do normal things on my own. It feels great. I needed this time alone today." I think they had some fun describing all the ways I had been inconsiderate, but I also know they understood where I was coming from. Mostly they were relieved that I had made it home in one piece.

All the same, Mom had to have the last word. "You do this again, Dwight, and I'll knock you silly." She needed to add one final exclamation point to the evening.

The next morning, I decided to take another ride on my own. I was completely at ease in the driver's seat; it felt like I had been driving every day for the past year. Tamika lived about twenty miles away, and I decided I would surprise her by driving to her apartment. I called her on my cell when I arrived and asked if she'd go for a ride with me. I wanted to show off, and I wanted her to be my first passenger.

We rode around for about a half hour, and I was filled with happiness. Tamika, however, didn't quite share my sentiments.

"Dwight, you better slow down now. You're still new to this, and if you're not careful, we'll have two people in a wheelchair."

I wasn't doing anything dangerous, but she had to get used to the idea that it was safe for me to drive. I soon learned that everybody was initially uncomfortable with me behind the wheel. It was a natural reaction, and they all needed a little time to see I could drive as safely as anybody else even though I couldn't use my feet. From that day on, I have been driving myself anywhere at any time under any condition.

I had long before decided that I wanted to make my experience count for something by telling my story in public. I wanted to talk about the dangers of drinking and driving, about the real-world consequences that a single bad decision can have on people's lives, and about how you can have a full and rewarding life even though you suffer from a disability. A local rep from Mothers Against Drunk Driving (MADD) had contacted me shortly before my second rehab stay and asked me to speak before a group of youngsters in Jackson. This was my first formal speech in front of a large group of people I didn't know, and I wanted it to be perfect. I prepared for many hours and rehearsed over and over the key points I wanted to make. I wanted to tell my story, but it wouldn't do much good unless I became a skilled public speaker. This would be my first test.

The presentation was in a large church auditorium with about three hundred people in attendance. Several buses and vans were parked outside, and people were there from Boys & Girls Clubs, church youth groups, and numerous other organizations from throughout the state. I was nervous because I was the only speaker that day, and I wanted to leave the kids with something to remember.

Before we started, I passed out several stacks of pictures to circulate during my presentation—pictures of my crushed car, of me in the ICU, of the accident scene with the police and EMTs, of me in rehab, of quadriplegics in rehab, and many, many more. There were kids there of all ages, and I was grateful to be speaking to youngsters instead of adults. I seem to be able to connect with kids, and the interaction is always joyful. Shortly after they were seated, the MADD rep gave a brief introduction, and I rolled onto the stage.

I smiled broadly and said, "How you doin'? Let's have some fun today." I started clapping to set a beat, then asked them to join me so I could rap along with the rhythm. They clapped in unison, and I started rapping an original song of mine.

> *Today we're gonna talk*
> *About not to drink and drive.*
> *Today we're gonna talk*
> *To keep yourself alive*
>
> *Today you'll see some pictures*
> *Of a car that's bent and crushed;*
> *Today you'll see some pictures*
> *And learn that drinking is more than just a rush.*
>
> *Today you'll walk away and wonder*
> *How I survived this thing at all,*
> *Today you'll hear a story and think: "My God, I never knew,"*
> *And hope and pray forever, that this is never you.*

This may not be the best rap in the world, but it did the trick. The kids knew I wrote it for them, and they loved it. They were clapping with me, and they knew I appreciated rap, something they enjoyed immensely. They sensed my effort and my respect for them. They were with me from the moment I started the rap until the Q&A session was over about ninety minutes later.

Tamika had come with me to hear the presentation, and she started crying about five minutes into it. All the memories were fresh in her mind, and she had lived every minute of this ordeal with me. It was still ongoing. The kids respected her tears, and it added weight to the talk. There were kids of all ages in attendance from third grade to college, and as the pictures got passed from person to person, I sometimes heard a gasp or a kid saying, "I can't believe he's alive."

I spoke for an hour. Though the topic was deadly serious, I sprinkled it with bits of humor. I talked about tipping over all the time in rehab and told the kids that the therapist said I was "gravity challenged." I talked about sharing football stories and lifting weights with Ryan and about how Rocky jumped into my lap when I finally got home. I told them about the agreement I had made with God to help other people like me and to show the world the damage that can be done by drinking and driving. My broader message was simple and somber: It's selfish to drink and drive. You put your own life at risk and can cause a lifetime of sorrow for people who love you. You also put the lives of other people at risk.

"You don't want to do to somebody else what Posey did to me," I said, and then I closed with, "When you drink, you can't think. It's just not worth it to drink and drive. Do the world a favor, keep yourself alive."

I didn't want to scare the kids—or at least, I didn't want to give them nightmares. But I did want them to leave with a graphic example of what one wrong decision can do. After I had finished speaking, I received a long standing ovation. The kids were honestly moved by my story, and they wanted to know more. I opened the floor for a Q&A session, and I learned very quickly that young kids ask the oddest and most direct questions. They were fascinated by the pictures and by my wheelchair, but they didn't quite know what to make of it all.

"Mr. Dwight, do you know my mama?" one girl asked. She wanted to know because her mother was in a wheelchair as well, and she assumed I must know her.

"Mr. Dwight, I can't believe you can drive. Who drove you here really?"

"Mr. Dwight, how much did your wheelchair cost?"

"Mr. Dwight, can you give me a ride in the wheelchair?"

"Mr. Dwight, how old was the man who hit you? Did the police put him in jail?"

"Mr. Dwight, how do you go to the bafroom?"

"Mr. Dwight, I ain't never gonna drive."

"Mr. Dwight, do you ever get a flat tire on your wheelchair?"

The questions were honest, and the kids were eager for me to keep talking. They needed time and information to process this strange experience.

The event was interesting for the kids and uplifting for me. I knew I wanted this to be the first of many presentations, and I was proud to have finally given a little back for all the care and love I had received during the past year. The scales were far from balanced, but I had at least taken my first step, and I planned to make telling my story a big part of my life in the future.

Shortly after my presentation, WAPT Television in Jackson called asking if they could interview me in my home and put my story on the evening news. I agreed immediately, and they sent an interviewer and two cameramen to my house the next day. They interviewed me at the kitchen table, asking questions for about a half hour. They also wanted to see me do things, so they filmed me getting into my standing frame, which is much like parallel bars in gymnastics. They filmed me as I rolled through various rooms in the house, and they took shots of me doing a transfer.

As the interview was coming to an end, the crew asked my Mom if she would take them to the actual site of the accident so they could shoot some footage there. The story appeared on the six o'clock and the ten o'clock news programs the following night. The three-minute segment opened with the scene of the accident. Three minutes was a big piece for a thirty-minute show, and the two newscasts reached tens of thousands of people. After it was over, I felt like a star was born. That star, however, was not me.

While the crew had been filming at my mom's house, I kept Rocky in a separate room so he wouldn't get in the way. He was not happy about being excluded, and he barked his annoyance every few minutes. Just as the interview was ending and the crew was getting ready to leave, I asked one of the cameramen to open the door and let him out. When he did, Rocky came running at me as fast as he could with his tiny feet going a mile a minute. He took a great leap onto my wheelchair and started licking my face. The crew caught this on film and ended both segments with Rocky showing his affection for his best buddy. Every call I got about the interview started out with comments about Rocky's antics. He had upstaged me and stolen the heart of every viewer. Rocky became a star in Hot Coffee, Mississippi, and people still talk about him today.

After my second brief stint at rehab, I felt stronger, more energetic, and more confident than I had in more than a year. It was evident to the people around me, and they began to recognize that I could do just about anything on my own. In one case, however, my independence caused some uncomfortable moments.

I suddenly started receiving odd phone calls, and I didn't know why.

"Dwight, I can't believe you're walking again. I'm so happy for you," one friend called to say.

Soon after, I got another call from my cousin. "Dwight, when did you start walking again? That's so great."

I received several calls like this every day for about a week, and I was dumbfounded. At first I feared it was a cruel prank, and I patiently explained to each caller that I was permanently paralyzed and couldn't walk. The rumor simply wasn't true. A few days later, we finally figured out the mystery.

After I got my driver's license, I began driving everywhere on my own. People were surprised at this, and they would honk and wave whenever they saw me behind the wheel. Some people didn't realize that paralyzed people can still drive, and apparently somebody saw me driving and assumed that if I could drive, I must be able to walk. We never learned who started the rumor, but the story got back to me that people saw me driving and thought I'd been cured. There was no malice in the rumor, and it was really the result of the community being happy and wishing me the best. It did prove, however, that many people had a lot to learn about people with disabilities.

Shortly after the "Oh my God, he can walk" rumor surfaced, Tamika came by after school. She had a more serious look on her face than normal. I wasn't sure what it meant, but I didn't think it would be a good thing.

"Dwight, where do you see our relationship going?" she asked. And if there was ever a question fraught with danger, this was it. I probably should have had an answer in my hip pocket, but all I could do was stammer my way through it. In retrospect, I realize I should have already thought long and hard about that question many months before, and I should have been able to say something without spurts and stutters. Tamika had been my emotional safety net, my port in a storm during a very rough period. Our relationship had grown deeper and deeper with each month, but I had been casual about it. I had been far too self-centered, and now she wanted answers. It was only fair.

In between the "uhms" and "ers" and the lengthy pauses, I managed to express honestly if not eloquently how much I loved her and how grateful I was to have her in my life. This past year had been psychologically and physically grueling, and I would never have survived it without her help every step of the way. I felt this in my heart, and I knew it in my mind. But I had never put it into proper words. Tamika had every right to think about her future. Were we a couple with a long-term future together, or were we two people with a deep friendship but separate lives ahead of us?

Tamika's timing was perfect, and it was clear she had given this a lot of thought. She had never tested me like this before, and she wouldn't have done it then unless she knew I was ready for it. At least sort of. I had improved so dramatically over the previous few months that it was time to think ahead. It was time to address the matter in a meaningful way.

This conversation happened in November of 2006, and I managed to stumble through it. Barely. But it served its purpose. Tamika is a no-nonsense person. Stay on task. Get the job done. I, on the other hand, am more happy-go-lucky, inclined to go with the moment, and generally less focused. But not this time. I started to think of what life would be without her, and it wasn't a happy picture. I loved Tamika, but I had been too busy thinking about myself to fully recognize her for the gift she was. She knew me when I was able-bodied before the accident, and she never balked once at my paralysis. I had seen many husbands and wives unable to withstand the strain of being married to a paralyzed spouse, even when they had been married before the paralysis. Tamika had seen me through the very worst of times, and I knew I could trust her feelings. I was now sure I could trust mine as well, and I came up with a plan.

My birthday is on December 21, and I decided to make it special that year. Tamika and I went out to dinner in Hattiesburg and got a hotel for the evening. I had everything planned and suggested we watch a movie in the room. I had brought a DVD with me, and said: "Tamika, will you get the movie out of that drawer? It's my birthday, so I get to choose the flick tonight." She wasn't thrilled with this deal because we don't share the same taste in movies, but she went along with it.

When Tamika opened the drawer, she saw a small box there and asked what it was.

I said, "Bring it here, Tamika. Let me see."

Knowing that something was up, she handed the box to me. I opened it, pulled out the ring, and said, "Tamika, I love you dearly and want to live with you forever. Will you marry me?"

She yelled out a big whoop—and then tried to get serious. "Dwight, of course I'll marry you, you big goof. What took you so long?"

We were both as happy as we'd ever been. She kissed me and said, "Oh, I've gotta make a call." She dialed the number and before the other person could say hello, she blurted: "Mama, guess what? Dwight just proposed. We're getting married, and I already have everything planned out," which was news to me. They chatted for a while and Tamika then proceeded to call all her other friends. She was exuberant…but then she finally remembered I was still there.

"Dwight," she said, "I've been waiting for this for a long time. I've loved you since long before the accident. You're just a dopey guy and never seemed to get it."

Well, I am just a dopey guy, but I was smart enough this time to get at least one thing right. I proposed on my birthday, which means I will never forget the date. I think that will spare me some grief in the years ahead. For a dopey guy, I thought my plan was brilliant.

This was a happy and extremely busy time for Tamika and me. She was teaching full time, planning a wedding, and helping me with my new role as a public speaker. On top of that, we knew we couldn't live with my mom after we got married, so we decided to have a house built. We purchased a few acres of land, which is very inexpensive in Mississippi, and started looking at house plans. It was more than Tamika wanted to deal with, so she made her own proposal.

"There's so much going on right now I can't keep up with it all. I trust you. Why don't you manage the house construction, and I'll plan the wedding?"

It sounded innocent enough, but I knew what she was up to. Tamika presented this as if it were a smart division of labor that would help us get everything done. The real truth, though, was that she just didn't trust my judgment. Each time she asked my opinion on something about the wedding, I inevitably picked the wrong option. She wanted me to feel important and tried to include me, but I never seemed to make the choice she had already settled upon. Her solution was to muscle me out of the wedding plans and have me occupy myself with the house. And that solution suited me just fine.

In fact, I was quite pleased with Tamika's suggestion. Even though I was thrilled to get married, I was just pretending to enjoy all the wedding preparations. I was much happier looking at house plans, talking things over with masons and framers, and keeping my fingers on the pulse of construction. I would make sure the home had all the ADA features I needed, like the wide doorways, accessible bathrooms, and lever knobs that my mom had had installed in her house. Of course, later on when it came time to decide on all the finishes, Tamika muscled me out of the picture again. Her trust went only so far. I wanted to make sure the house was built well and had a room with a large flat screen TV so I could watch the football games, but I couldn't pick matching tile or the right kind of curtains if my life depended on it. Like any good manager, Tamika seems to know all my strengths and weaknesses—and she never lets me get in over my head.

After my segments on the WAPT evening news in Jackson, calls started coming in fast and furious, none more important than the one I received from Chinika Hughes. Chinika had graduated from my alma mater, the University of Southern Mississippi, and was a writer for the university newspaper. She had many media contacts and dreams of starting her own public relations company. She called to interview me for the campus paper, but she also had something else in mind. Chinika wanted me to become a client. I had never considered having a publicist before, but I was getting so many calls to appear at different events that I knew I could use the help.

Chinika was full of energy, enthusiasm, and good ideas. She wanted my story to be known throughout the South and was eager to get started. We spoke several times, and Tamika and I met her and her husband for dinner one evening. Not long after, Chinika called me with a proposal.

"You know my opinion," she said. "I think your story is a big deal. It's inspiring, and it can help save lives. It can also give people in your situation hope for the future. It touches many people at many levels, and it can make a difference." She paused. "I have several ideas and a plan we can implement. Are you ready to listen?"

I was skeptical but interested. Chinika wanted to promote a tour of inspirational speeches under the theme "Before You Drink, Think Dwight." We could team up with the Mississippi Department of Transportation, the Attorney General's office, and organizations like MADD. She wanted to focus initially on middle schools and high schools in the state, including her alma mater, South Pike High School. She could arrange numerous radio and television interviews and help me set up a schedule of appearances.

And then she made a remarkably generous offer. "Dwight, I don't want to charge you anything for this work. I am not doing this to feather my own nest. Your success will help my business, of course, but the important point is to get the story out. I want to be part of it, and this is a chance for us to put our good intentions into good actions. Good thoughts alone aren't worth a dime. We have to make a plan and execute it."

I was intrigued and excited by her words. I did what I always do when presented with a new idea. "Chinika," I said, "I'm happy to think about your offer. Give me a few days, let me figure out what questions I have, and I'll get back to you shortly." I did just that. I called her back a week later, discussed some details, and told her I was onboard. We worked together for the next three years.

Chinika soon contacted WDAM, Channel 7 out of Hattiesburg. She arranged an interview with the host of "The Morning Show," a very popular program in Southern Mississippi. Many people start their day with this show, and it has a long reach in the lower half of the state. WDAM invited me in for an interview, asking me to arrive at five o'clock in the morning. I drove there with Tamika, Mom, and my stepfather, and the WDAM staff quickly ushered us onto the set. We watched the newscasters and meteorologist prepare for their segments and took in the flurry of activity around us. I had never seen a live television program from an inside perspective, and I was taken with how much was happening at the same time. It looks quite easy to a viewer, but there are a great many moving parts that have to fit together with little margin for error.

"The Morning Show" host, Sharon Stahler, was a celebrity in the area. Because she sat on a couch on a raised platform, they had built a temporary ramp so I could roll up and speak with her. The interview was conversational and felt comfortable even though there were cameras moving about and people doing various tasks in the background.

Ms. Stahler gave a brief overview of my background and the accident and then turned to me. "Welcome, Dwight. We're so pleased you could join us this morning and share your story. Let's start with this. You were physically active all your life and always an excellent athlete. You were a high school football player with dreams of playing in college and perhaps beyond. What were the biggest challenges you faced after your accident?"

"Ms. Stahler, the accident was a life changer at every level. I was a teacher and had just started my first year as an assistant football coach when a drunk driver crashed into the back of my car. You can see the results. I coded after the accident, and the doctors didn't expect me to survive. For the first few weeks, my greatest challenge was simply taking one breath after the other and surviving long enough to see the next day. Over time, the biggest challenge was to keep my hopes alive and not become depressed. That sounds easier than it is, and I never would have made it here without the constant love and encouragement of my family and community. Everybody pitched in to help."

"You were hit by a drunk driver. Can you tell us something about him and what you feel about him?" she asked.

"Well, the man who hit me had been cited on four prior occasions for DUI. He was drunk again on the afternoon of the accident. He was driving too fast on a rainy day and simply drove into the back of my car on Highway 84. I went down a gully and crashed into a tree. His actions turned my life upside down and impacted the lives of many other people as well. I went through various stages of anger, acceptance, compassion, and finally forgiveness. I can't change what happened, and I have to stay focused on getting better, not on getting even. I try not to think about him. I let the hatred go a long time ago."

The initial interview went on like this for about six minutes before the show broke for commercials. "Stay tuned, people. We'll have more with Dwight after these messages. You won't want to miss it," she said. I was surprised by this because I didn't expect them to do two segments with me, but they did. I was comfortable and enjoying myself, and Ms. Stahler told me during the break that everything was going great. After we got back on the air, they did the weather report and a brief set of news items before returning to me.

"Welcome back. We're here with Dwight Owens talking about the accident that put him in a wheelchair for the rest of his life." She then turned to me and said, "We chatted for several minutes about the accident and what you've gone through since then. What are your future plans?"

"My goal is to make the accident have meaning, to make it count for something. I want to share my story and work with people in a similar situation. I've been speaking publicly and trying to educate kids on the dangers of drinking and driving. It has been very rewarding for me."

Ms. Stahler then closed by asking, "What's the most important message you want to leave with our viewers?"

I paused because I didn't want to sound angry. Finally I said, "My message is this: Drinking and driving is selfish. Period. You can kill or maim yourself and cause endless grief for the people you love and who love you. Worse yet, you might kill or maim innocent victims. I want the viewers to look at me and ask themselves if it's really worth it. I can tell you, it's not."

We wrapped up, and I felt great. Tamika gave me a kiss, which is my favorite reward. Mom said, "Dwight, I raised myself a beautiful son. I'm proud of you." WDAM did two six-minute segments, and the interview was the main feature of the day. I didn't do it because I'm a publicity hound or because I wanted sympathy. I did it because I wanted to honor my promise to God to make a difference. I felt I had, and I felt that I was ready to take off in a new career.

For the next week it seemed like the phone rang every ten minutes. One of my former students called and said, "Mr. Owens, I was brushin' my teeth when I heard your voice on TV. I pulled the toothbrush out my face and ran to watch. You looked good. It was great to see you."

Of course, I got lots of teasing from my family as well.

"Dwight, I'll never understand how a knucklehead like yourself ever got a gig on "The Morning Show." TV programming is heading down the drain fast."

"Sir Dwight, will you be joining us at dinner this evening or are you dining with the Queen?"

It went on like this for a week, but I just rolled with it. "Voncarie," I'd answer, "not only will I be joining you for dinner tonight, I'll be cooking it. You better show up on time."

Outside of sports, my favorite hobby is cooking. I consider myself a master on the grill, and I am completely at home in a kitchen. My special dish is banana pudding, and shortly after my second rehab, Mom asked me, "Can you cook a batch of your famous banana pudding for our guests tomorrow?" The question startled me for two reasons. First, I didn't know we were having guests. Second, I suddenly realized that I had not cooked a single meal since my accident.

Mom worked full time as a welder and often put in extra hours without a word of complaint. Tamika worked full time as a teacher and always put in many extra hours. I sat full time as an invalid and sometimes put in extra hours doing that. After a full workday, Mom would come home every evening and cook dinner. I am sometimes slow to recognize the obvious, but it finally struck me like a sharp slap in the face that I had not been carrying my own weight. Nobody expected me to yet, but I could certainly help out, and I should have been doing most of the cooking chores for the past few months.

"Mom, that's a great idea. Not only will I make the pudding, let me take care of dinner. It's about time, don't you think?"

Mom smiled broadly and said: "Dwight, I taught you everything I know about cooking, so I'm sure it will be a fine dinner."

It was. I was embarrassed that I hadn't started helping with the cooking months back, but I vowed to make up for my failings. We were having some family members over for a casual dinner, so it wasn't a big event. The big deal was that I finally started taking some of the load off Mom and Tamika.

This was the first time I had to maneuver around the kitchen for a long period of time. It was hard and frustrating, but it was also fun. Hard because the kitchen is much less open than other areas of the house, and I had to be very precise when rolling my chair. Hard because I had to reach for everything with my gripper, even things off the top shelf of the cabinet. I refused to accept help from anybody because I would have to do this on my own if I was going to cook for the family in the future. It was a mini-rehab for me. The meal took longer than normal to prepare, but the banana pudding was a hit, and everybody enjoyed the dinner. And since then, for the past three years, I've been doing most of the cooking for the family.

My days during that time were full and rewarding. Tamika and I were together at every opportunity, and she talked about the wedding plans all the time. When she finally got quiet, I talked about the construction of our new home. I was back in the swing of things, and it felt like I had more than a full-time job. I was busy either speaking at schools, rehab centers, and churches, or preparing for an upcoming presentation. I was also doing some other work on the side.

I loved teaching and deeply regretted that my career had been cut so abruptly short. I knew I wasn't physically up to going back full time, but there was a consolation prize. I had often tutored in college, and I was the "go-to" guy in my church when kids needed help with math, computers, and technical things. I once again offered my services at church, and the word spread quickly. I soon had students at my house several days a week and usually on weekends, and they were from all around the town, not just our church. I never accept payment for these services because the church and the broader community had been so loyal and steadfast in their support of me. I was grateful for the chance to give a little back, and it seemed the least I could do to express my appreciation. It did, however, get a bit out of hand on occasion.

Sometimes I would return from a speaking engagement and find a couple of students on my porch. Or, I would be preparing to go out to dinner with Tamika, and the doorbell would ring. People were dropping off their kids without any notice, and I couldn't just leave them alone in my house. It felt great to be helping and making a difference, but it was getting out of control. I finally put the word out that everybody was welcome, and I would do my best for any students who needed help, but they had to call first. They couldn't just show up whenever the spirit moved them. The community had gotten so used to me just being in the house that they didn't understand that I had other commitments. By this point, however, I was on the road giving presentations several days a week, and I couldn't just stop whatever I was doing to tutor. But I still manage to find time to tutor every week, usually two or three times.

Life was getting better almost by the day, but not everything was perfect. A full night's sleep, for example, is impossible for me. I have to wake up every three hours to turn over in order to prevent bedsores and damage to my circulation. Everybody else does this naturally when they're sleeping, but paralyzed people can't. The solution is to set the alarm clock, wake up, and roll myself over. It's a process that takes a couple of minutes, and it's a nuisance. I never sleep more than three hours without interruption, and I'm sometimes a bit droopy or cranky as a result.

The other thing is phantom pain. It never goes away, and even though I have no feeling in my legs if I bump them against something, the phantom pain still makes me feel like my legs are being stung by a swarm of bees all the time. It's not the gentle tingling you get when your arm falls asleep. It's about five times more intense, and it never stops. The discomfort is with me every minute of my waking life. It is a common condition for paralyzed people. Some choose to visit acupuncturists or doctors who specialize in pain management to find relief, but no solution seems to last very long. I just accept that this pain will always be there and then try to ignore it. Some days I'm better at it than others.

Not long after my appearance on WDAM, I got a call from Chinika saying she had booked me at South Pike High School in Magnolia, Mississippi, about 150 miles away. She was excited about this because she had graduated from South Pike and knew the principal and many of the teachers. This would be the official start of our "Before You Drink, Think Dwight" tour. Chinika and Superintendent Sanford had contacted MADD and a local car dealership called Woolwine's Auto to sponsor the event. They graciously paid for five hundred t-shirts with a picture of me in a football uniform, a picture of my crushed car, and then a powerful shot of me in my wheelchair. They had logos of Woolwine's and MADD on the side. And on the back, we had the motto "Before You Drink, Think Dwight" along with a series of pictures representing my life in high school, as a teacher, in the ICU, and in my wheelchair.

I worked on my presentation for many hours because I knew just how important this was to Chinika. I also had a surprise in mind. The event took place in May of 2007, and the entire junior and senior classes—over five hundred students—were in attendance. The school had dedicated two full periods to the event, and they scheduled it just before the junior and senior proms. The school administration didn't want to dampen the kids' enthusiasm or detract from their enjoyment of the proms, but they did want them to exercise caution and moderation. One look at me would do the trick.

The school had been planning the event for several weeks, and they invited newspaper and broadcast media to attend. They teamed up with the Mississippi Department of Transportation, which placed a car that had been crushed in a drunk driving accident in front of the school. All the kids in the junior and senior classes saw the vehicle and learned its story. The officer in charge explained how this was the work of a drunken driver and told them about the deaths that resulted. It was a chilling sight. By the time the two classes were assembled, they were eager to hear my story, and I was eager to tell it.

After a brief introduction, I rolled on stage and just looked at them for a full minute. The auditorium was silent, nervous. I was a strange sight, and things got stranger yet when I said, "I want you to clap and help me set the beat. When I say Youth, you say Power. When I say Youth, you say Power." I glanced to the side of the stage and saw Chinika with a startled look on her face. She wasn't sure what would happen next, but she was certainly fearful. I had not told her about this part of my speech beforehand.

I started clapping a beat and began a rap.

Drugs are like a weapon on the path to kill
They search for youth, no time to feel
Alcohol and drugs cannot make a man
Listen to me, begin to understand

That life is short, don't mess it up
Don't listen to the boys saying "Girl, wass up?"
Don't fall into the trap cause you'll get hurt
'Cause welfare's full, you need to work

Keep your mind on school, and school on your mind
Don't be stupid, don't run out of time
Control yourself, every minute, every hour
When I say Youth, you say Power

Youth…Power
Youth…Power
Youth…Power,

You have the power, now make the most of it!

I rapped this in a strong voice, and the kids loved it. They yelled out "POWER" louder and louder each time I said "Youth," and they got caught up in the spirit of the moment. From that point on, I knew I had their attention. I spoke for about an hour and received a standing ovation when I was done. We then went through about a half hour of Q&A, and the questions from the high school students and adults were quite different from those I had been getting from youngsters.

Since then, I've noticed some themes in the questions I get. First, everybody wants to know about Posey. Questions about Posey are the part I like least about these presentations, but everybody wants to know what happened to him. It seems to close the circle.

"Did they put him in jail for the rest of his life?" A long time, but he'll probably get out before he dies.

"Do you hate him, Mr. Owens?" No. Forgiveness is the best path to recovery, and we can't waste our lives with hatred. I let it go.

"Has he ever contacted you, written you a letter, or called to apologize?" No.

Another major line of questioning involves depression.

"Did you ever consider suicide, Mr. Owens?" No, but many people do. Such a dramatic and painful change in circumstances can crush the spirit of even the strongest person. This is a big problem for paralyzed people.

"Did you ever get depressed personally, and how did you deal with it?" I don't know if a psychiatrist would say I was clinically depressed at points along the way, but I had my down periods. I make it my job to accentuate the positive. I am blessed with a loving family, a beautiful fiancée, and a belief that God only gives us challenges we can handle. I work hard to keep a smile on my face.

"Do you know any people like you who committed suicide?" Yes.

The third line of inquiry is always positive, and it involves questions about life in a wheelchair and dealing with a major disability.

"Can you drive?" Yes.

"Can you have sex?" Yes.

"Are there any other medical problems from being in a wheelchair?" Many.

"How should I deal with a person with a disability?" Treat them respectfully and like anybody else.

"What are the biggest problems you face?" It's a long list, but keeping my spirit up is the most important.

"How do you deal with people staring at you all the time?" I smile and try to put them at ease.

And many, many others. I love these questions because they give me a chance to explain that people with disabilities are people first. They love their families; they are as intellectually and often as physically active as able-bodied people; and in most cases, they want to be treated like everybody else. Then I usually add: "But we do enjoy our special parking privileges."

The presentation at South Pike was a hit, and Chinika felt triumphant.

"Dwight, I can't believe you didn't tell me about that rap. You scared the hell out of me, but it was great," she said enthusiastically. The speech was fun, but the day was far from over. I made my presentation in the morning and then joined the faculty for lunch in the cafeteria. The teachers peppered me with questions, and I talked about how to deal with people with disabilities, about the ADA, about MADD, and about fifty other topics.

When we broke up after lunch, I spent the afternoon in individual freshman and sophomore classes speaking for about twenty minutes to groups of twenty or thirty students at a time. I was there until the final bell rang for the day, and I felt a great sense of joy and accomplishment when it was over. On the drive home, I reflected on the fact that not much more than one year ago, I had coded and the doctors had given me no chance of survival. Now I was speaking to hundreds of kids at a time and sharing my story every week. I was proud. I was energized. Most of all, I was grateful. Grateful the doctors were wrong, and grateful that God had given me a second chance to do something worthwhile. The "Before You Drink, Think Dwight" tour was underway, and I planned to make the most of it.

11

A DAY TO REMEMBER

Tamika and I selected November 17, 2007, for our wedding date, which gave us almost a year to get ready. We needed every minute of it. Although Tamika had taken charge of the wedding while I was responsible for the home construction, she had by far the tougher job.

"Dwight, we were gonna have a small wedding party, and we're at ten people now. It's getting too big," she said.

"Tamika," I answered, "whose fault is that? You're in charge of the wedding."

She didn't find this answer amusing and gave me a growl in response. I was the one who had asked for extra people to be part of the wedding party.

"Well, it would help if your brothers and the other guys in the wedding party at least got fitted for their tuxedos," she said. Tamika was annoyed because the women had gotten fitted in the first month and now we were six months into planning and none of the guys had shown up yet. They were all happy to be part of the proceedings, but they weren't quite as motivated as Tamika wanted them to be. "Tell Cedrick and Voncarie to get themselves down to the tux place," she said. "I don't need to be worrying about them for the next few months." And from her tone, I knew I had better give them a call.

Of course, Cedrick and Voncarie knew what was going on and wanted to have some fun with it.

"Dwight, you're already taking orders from Tamika. It's good to start early and get some practice," Cedrick suggested.

Voncarie took his cue and jumped in. "Big brother, we'll do more than that for you. We'll even help you pick out a pretty dress for yourself. You'll need to look sharp at the wedding."

These two would never have dared to stand up to Tamika like this, but they enjoyed giving me a hard time. What are brothers for? I just smiled and said, "Okay then. I'll ask Tamika to give you a call." That seemed to improve their spirit of cooperation. A week later, all ten of the guys in the wedding party had been fitted.

Early on in the planning process, Tamika and I made a key decision about the wedding. Neither of us drinks, and we wanted the wedding to be alcohol-free.

"I think our guests will understand," Tamika said. "It would be horrible if somebody drank too much and had an accident on the way home. We don't need liquor to make this wedding special."

I agreed. "Given my situation, alcohol would send the wrong message. Besides, I'd prefer everybody to be clear-headed." I knew our guests would understand and even appreciate our choice.

Tamika did everything to make the wedding perfect. She asked her cousin and close friend to sing "When I First Saw You" from Dreamgirls. She arranged for the photographer and videographer; she selected the reception site and planned the menu with the caterer; she arranged for a violinist at the wedding and a DJ at the reception; she chose the flower arrangements; and she worked down her to-do list with a laser focus. When you put Tamika on a task, she doesn't dawdle. This wedding was going to be everything she wanted, and I watched with admiration as she arranged detail after detail.

The day before the wedding, my brothers and a few friends decided we needed our own pre-wedding celebration.

"Dwight, get ready. We're leaving for the Golden Moon in twenty minutes," Cedrick said. I was caught off guard but willing to play along. The Golden Moon is a casino in Philadelphia, Mississippi, about 150 miles from where we lived. The five of us piled into my truck, and I had the honor of driving the festive group to my bachelor party. The guys knew I didn't want a big celebration, so we just went out to dinner, played some cards and slots, and decided to call it a night around one o'clock in the morning. We'd get back before four o'clock, get a few hours' sleep, and be set for the big day with no harm done.

Cedrick drove back, and we were all in good spirits but tired. The evening had been a lot of fun, but no plan ever works perfectly. When we were about seventy miles from home, I noted the gas gauge was getting low.

"Cedrick, you need to pull over and fill up the tank," I said.

Cedrick, who never lacks for confidence however misplaced it may be, answered, "Dwight, don't worry your pretty little face. I got this under control. We have plenty of gas to get home."

I didn't agree and pushed the point. "I think I know my own truck better than you do. We might make it, but we might not. No need to take the risk."

Cedrick now felt his judgment had been challenged, and he was not about to budge. It became a point of honor. "Dwight, you worry about your wedding night. I'll worry about the driving," he said flatly.

Voncarie enjoys watching Cedrick and me tangle every now and again, and he was not about to weigh in with an opinion. Twenty minutes later the truck sputtered to a halt. It was pushing four o'clock in the morning, and everybody was ready to be home.

"Cedrick, you dope. I thought they might have taught your dumb self something in the Navy. Apparently not. I'm gonna miss my own wedding because of you."

The others joined in. "Good job, Cedrick. Good thing we have you to make these decisions for us," said Lee, one of my closest friends.

And Voncarie wasn't about to let the matter go, either. "Cedrick, some of us use that growth on top of our shoulders for thinking. You might try it some time."

The good news was that we had managed to roll into the parking lot of a small diner that had a gas pump outside. It wasn't open yet, and we could only hope it was still in business. Fortunately, a couple of people showed up a little before six o'clock, and we were able to buy some gas and get back on the road. We pulled in the driveway around seven o'clock in the morning, and since we had to be at the church in a few hours, I didn't bother going to sleep. I also didn't tell Tamika about the night's hijinks. She was stressed enough already and didn't need to know how I'd almost been a no-show for the wedding. As for Cedrick, he's the best brother anybody could ever have. That day, however, I would have gladly traded him for a bullfrog.

The wedding was everything we'd hoped for. It was a gorgeous autumn day and everybody was in a happy mood. The violinist played a haunting tune, and the two singers were stunning. I promised myself I wouldn't cry no matter what, but when I finally saw Tamika walking down the aisle toward me, my eyes filled with tears. This made Tamika start crying as well, which in turn made Mom and several others start daubing tissues at their eyes. We finally got ourselves composed, and we said our vows without incident. Tamika's preacher, Reverend Jaymar Jackson, conducted the ceremony at New Hope Baptist Church, and he loomed over the crowd. The attendees applauded in appreciation when the reverend pronounced us husband and wife.

For the week leading up to the wedding, I told Tamika I had a plan.

"Tamika, after we say our vows and the preacher says, 'You may kiss the bride,' I'm gonna whisk you into my arms and give you the biggest, longest smooch you've ever seen," I said.

Tamika would have none of it. "If you make a spectacle out of this, that's the only kiss you're gonna get," she said.

We went back and forth with this on several occasions, so when the reverend finally said those magical words, I motioned at her with my finger and said, "Come here, Darling." I could see in Tamika's eyes that she knew I was up to no good. She came just close enough so that I couldn't quite reach her, leaned over, and gave me a peck on the lips.

The guests knew something was up and started chiding Tamika. "Give him a real kiss, Tamika," one person called out. The guests started booing in good humor, and I sat there trying to look like the aggrieved victim. Tamika came back, wrapped her arms around me, and made up for the little peck she had given me moments before. The crowd laughed and applauded, and we got an early start on the reception festivities.

The reception was delightful, and when it came time to dance with the bride, we did a group dance instead. The DJ had everybody laughing throughout the afternoon, and when we approached the end, the videographer went from person to person to record a message from each of them. We got all the usual best wishes, but some were more humorous than others.

"Tamika, you take good care of this boy. And make sure you have a 'date night' at least once a month," one guest offered.

"Dwight, you make sure you let Tamika win sometimes when you're playing chess. Remember, a happy wife is a happy life," another said.

"Dwight, memorize the phrase 'Yes, dear,' and use it often. You'll be glad you did," said another guest.

When it was all finally over, Tamika and I drove to our new home, looked at it for a few minutes before entering, and spent our first night there together. We had decided to postpone our honeymoon, but this was the best ending we could imagine for the best day we had ever had.

12

A LIFE OF PUBLIC SERVICE

The "Before You Drink, Think Dwight" tour was off to a running start, and I wanted to keep the momentum going. The tour was receiving extensive broadcast and written coverage and lots of interest from schools across Mississippi and organizations supporting the disabled community. That's how I first met Eddie Jones, who co-founded the Southern Mississippi Public Accessibility Association (SMPAA) some twenty years ago.

Eddie had been in a wheelchair for over four decades and had become a tireless advocate for people with disabilities. To this day, he strives to make businesses and especially government facilities ADA compliant. SMPAA hosts a program called Walk With Me, held annually in Hattiesburg, Mississippi. Eddie thought my voice would add another dimension to the event, and he wanted me to be part of it.

"We haven't met, yet, but I know this about you, Dwight," he said. "You need to be the keynote speaker at our event this October. I won't take 'no' for an answer." I didn't know him, but I liked him right away. He was earnest, enthusiastic, and clearly a bundle of energy.

But still, I had some questions. "Mr. Jones, let's slow down a little," I said. "I need to know a lot more about you and your organization before I commit to anything. Who are you and what do you do?"

Eddie laughed and took his cue. A compelling man, Eddie told me how he had become paralyzed, how he founded the SMPAA to support people with disabilities, and how his organization had made an impact throughout Southern Mississippi. Eddie was impossible to resist. I agreed to be the event's keynote speaker, and I have been a member of SMPAA's Advisory Board ever since.

SMPAA's annual Walk With Me campaign is a big deal. It engages the community and asks participants to become disabled for a period of time. We put blindfolds on people and have them walk with a guide. We have them wear Mickey Mouse ears to simulate life for a deaf person, and we put able-bodied people in wheelchairs and give them some chores to do. They have to wheel up ramps, maneuver in tight spaces, and try to reach things with a gripper. In our most recent event we had a wheelchair challenge in which people competed in a mile-long race. My cousin Greg was beaming when he came in second, but most people gave up exhausted after a few hundred yards. Organizations like MADD, D.A.R.E., L.I.F.E., AmeriCorps, SMPAA, and others gather to educate the public about disabilities, and it's almost like a fall festival. We attract local and national politicians, prominent business people, and dignitaries and celebrities from across the state and beyond. There are always media personalities and media outlets in attendance. In 2007, SMPAA held the event at the Saenger Theater, which is an old-style venue from the 1920s. It is the crown jewel of the town. The audience was ready to hear a story, and it seemed like all eyes were on me.

I was more than a bit nervous after I learned about the reach of the event, but I was excited to be a part of it. At least for one day, the community would be focused on the challenges facing people with disabilities, and this was my chance to show that we are people first. We are not defined by our disabilities. Everybody has challenges. Ours are a little more visible than most.

I drove to the theater the day before to get the lay of the land and make sure it was wheelchair accessible. It was. I could easily get on stage and strut my stuff. On the following day, the theater was bustling with activity. The street had been cordoned off for buses bringing people with disabilities to the theater. Camera people were filming the day's events, and reporters were busily taking notes. I realized quickly that many in the audience already knew my story. They were eager, however, to hear me tell it in my own words. For a fleeting moment, a jolt of panic shot through me, and I felt myself wishing I could become invisible. I kissed my dog tag, which has the Lord's Prayer on it, and looked to Tamika for support. I gathered my composure, found my voice, and regained my courage. The moment of panic passed, and by the time the mayor completed his opening remarks, I was ready to roll.

Since this was largely an adult audience, I didn't start with a rap. I spoke more somberly than usual, but I still sprinkled the talk with many humorous anecdotes. I talked about how the therapists would try to knock me over in rehab by throwing dodge balls at me—and how they were very successful in the beginning. Anecdotes like this always provide a welcome relief from the seriousness of the topic, and they put people at ease. They also remind everyone of just how normal and accessible I am.

Of course, I also talked about the accident, about Posey, about tipping over like a toy clown that bounces up and down when you punch it, and about the importance of the ADA for people like me. We want to participate in the world around us and make a positive contribution in our careers. All we need is a little help, not much.

"And darn it," I said at the close of the speech, "Stay out of our parking spots. You can walk an extra fifty feet."

This brought laughter and applause and marked the end of the formal presentation. The day was joyful, and it presented people with disabilities not as victims but as individuals who are normal in every respect except for their one visible challenge. The audience enthusiastically clapped and whistled their appreciation, and I felt like I had added one more block to the foundation of disability awareness we were trying to build.

I had a smile on my face for the entire week following—not because my speech had been well received, but because the whole event was promoted and executed in such a positive light. It received extensive television and radio coverage, and there were reports of it in local papers for several days. I was already pumped for and thinking ahead to my next speech because I was heading back to Collins Middle School. My school. The presentation for SMPAA was like kicking the extra point in a game where I had just scored the winning touchdown.

Just two years before this presentation, I was preparing to teach Math and Special Education at Collins Middle School, and I was also an assistant football coach for Collins High. I had attended both these schools as a youngster, and I was thrilled to be coming back as a teacher. Fate, however, intervened. I was coming back now…but not as a member of the faculty.

I had spoken with Ike Sanford, the school superintendent, and Coach Jackson. They made sure all the arrangements were clear and well defined. They let the students know ahead of time what the assembly was all about, and they dedicated the day to me. The school reserved the last two periods of the day for the speech, which indicated how big an event this was for them and me. It was more like a pep rally than a speech, and all six hundred kids and faculty were gathered in the gymnasium. They started whistling and clapping loudly when I arrived and stood up out of their seats. I knew many of the students and teachers personally, and I heard one student yell out, "Lookin' good, Mr. Owens! We thought you were a goner."

The student body was charged with excitement and happy to see me doing well. I could feel the electricity, the kids' personal investment in me. They all knew my story in detail—the accident, Posey, rehab, and how I finally made my way back into public. Most of them had seen me around town; they even know what vehicle I drove. I felt like I was coming home, and I loved it.

The school had invited a representative from MADD to join us, and she gave a brief presentation and then turned the podium over to Coach Jackson. He kicked things off in a fun way and talked about how I was in the Collins High School Hall of Fame. He talked about my play on the football field and how I was a member of the Beta Club, the top academic club at Collins High.

"Jocks are smart, they just don't show it all the time," he joked. He went on to tell the kids about how I was in the gym every day and could bench press more than any of the other football players. Then he joked that I could tackle like a mad man. "Mr. Beta always had a smile on his face, but no running backs ever smiled when he got his arms around them. The only direction he would let them go was backwards," said Coach Jackson. "And Dwight was already an honorary assistant coach in high school. He would help us run drills for the offensive line and then turn around and run some drills on defensive line."

Finally, it was my turn to come to the podium. The students were already in a festive mood, so I started with a rap. The kids always enjoy this because they get to participate. Their voices were booming at the end as I got into the final lines.

"When I say YOUTH, you say POWER. When I say YOUTH, you say POWER."

They were stomping and cheering and relishing the moment.

The theme of my speech was "Good Decisions." I talked about my accident, rehab, and the consequences of drinking and driving, but the broader goal was to ask the students to think before they act. You don't have to use drugs just because somebody else is. You don't need to drink just because other people do. Use that incredible brain you have and make your own decisions. Be responsible for your own actions and help your classmates do the same. I approached this message without being preachy. That never works. I provided lots of stories and anecdotes to drive the point home, knowing that one example is worth a month full of sermons.

When I wrapped up the speech, I told the kids about a package I received shortly after my lengthy rehabilitation. It was a bundle of over fifty letters from students there at Collins and players on the football team. I thanked them for the hard work and effort they put into them, and explained how I still read them. They bring me a smile every time I pull a letter out of the envelope.

I closed the speech with a poem I had written. It was titled "Hang In There," and it described the pressures kids face and ways they can deal with them. As I finished, Mr. Sanford gave me the biggest smile ever and raised his thumb high in the air. He had been a big part of my journey. He was one of the first to suggest that I take my story to the public. I'm sure he was inwardly proud of the good deed he had done. After the speech, the students gave me a large gift basket of goodies filled with cheese, crackers, assorted candies, and other treats. I then had a chance to meet with many of the teachers. I told them how grateful I was that they had donated so many of their sick days to me. It made all the difference in the world, and I could not have made it without them. I wanted to make sure they knew once again how much I appreciated their generosity.

After the speech at Collins, Tamika and I went out to dinner for a "date night." We make a point of dedicating at least one night a month to ourselves, and we make it a special event. We decided to treat ourselves to a long, leisurely dinner at a restaurant we had wanted to visit for a long time. The restaurant is located on the top of a hill, and since the parking lot was full, I had to park on the street. The slope was steep, but I managed to wheel myself up the hill on my own. Over dinner, we talked about the speech at Collins, reminisced about our teaching days at Laurel High, and simply enjoyed each other's company.

As we were heading back to the truck, Tamika asked, "Dwight, this hill is pretty steep. Why don't you let me hold the handles on the wheelchair and help roll you down?"

I was annoyed by the question and brushed her suggestion off. "Tamika, you know better than that. There's no problem here. I can do this."

My confidence sometimes exceeds my capability, and I didn't realize quite how steep the hill was. Shortly after starting our downward trek, I lost control of the wheelchair and started speeding down the hill. I couldn't stop the chair because it was moving so fast and I got rubber burns on my hands when I tried to slow the tires. I turned my head, lifted my arms, and gave

Tamika a huge smile. I then let out a whoop. I knew I was going to crash into something—probably one of the cars on the side of the road or one in the parking lot at the bottom of the hill. All I could do was laugh and hope for the best. Tamika understood what I was thinking and started laughing with me. We would pick up the pieces afterwards.

The chair kept picking up speed, and Tamika was running as fast as she could to catch up. The wheelchair made it to the bottom of the hill where I slammed into the front tire of a parked car. I was dazed and bruised from the impact, but I was not seriously injured…unless you count the wound to my ego. I smiled at the irony of the situation, thinking I had been injured many times before when I didn't deserve it. This time, when I did, I got off scot-free. Maybe God was balancing the scales. Tamika caught up moments later, breathless and fearful of what she would find. She wrapped her arms around me and started laughing when she saw I was okay.

"Honey, I know you can do everything on your own," she said. "But that doesn't mean everything. It means most things, you big goof."

I was humbled by the experience and realized once again that I have two main enemies in life. Overconfidence and steep hills.

Among the presentations I have made along the way, many have been at correctional facilities, and my first was in Lamar County, Mississippi. It was not what I expected.

One of the managers at Lamar attended an earlier presentation I had made at Jones County Community College, where there were more than a thousand people in attendance. He thought I could make an impression on the inmates and asked me to speak at the correctional facility. When the day arrived for me to speak, I was a bit nervous because this would not be my normal crowd.

I think I expected to be on a stage speaking before a large group of people who couldn't care less about me or my story. Since they would not be there of their own free will, I thought I would receive a chilly, uninterested reception. But when I got to the facility, things were not quite what I imagined. They took me to a small conference room, and then about twenty-five people in orange jumpsuits walked in and surrounded me. The room could only seat about fifteen, so many of the inmates had to stand. There were blacks and whites, men and women, and a few of them were no more than two feet away from me. My heart was pounding furiously. I felt threatened. They had tattoos on their arms and faces, scraggly beards, and a demeanor that would frighten any sane person. I was sane, and I was scared. There was one unarmed guard by the door for security, and I thought we needed about ten.

I started talking about my life before the accident. I was filled with optimism and dreams for the future. I was about to do the two things I loved most in the world, teach and coach football. I then set the scene and described Herman Posey. My car, my body, and my dreams were all shattered into a million pieces all because of the selfish, thoughtless act of a drunk. I didn't mince words, and I stressed the unfairness of the situation. I was crippled, and Posey had nothing worse than a flat tire.

I then turned to the bigger picture. God gives all of us challenges, and success in life depends on how you face them. Some people grow up in broken homes or are victims of physical or sexual abuse. Some people grow up in poverty and others fall prey to drugs or alcohol. Some end up in jail because of a single bad decision they made in their youth. You can't undo the past, and it helps nobody to dwell on it. The better route is to accept it, put it behind you, and build a future for yourself. This might sound like a sermon you'd hear from the sternest of preachers, but the inmates were fascinated. They hung on my every word, and I heard sniffles and saw people drying their eyes as I spoke. This was not the reaction I expected.

After I was done, the inmates asked question after question for almost an hour, and they were genuinely moved by my willingness to spend the time with them. One woman said, "Mr. Owens, I am so sorry for all you gone through. We love you for coming here."

I fought to keep back my own tears. "I was a bit afraid to do this at first," I answered. "But I am so grateful to be here. God wants us to rise above our problems and do something worthwhile in our lives. You have your own set of challenges, and you have the talent and brainpower to turn things around. I'm on your side and wish you only the best."

When we were done, I received hugs and handshakes from each of the inmates. I realized how wrong I had been in judging them so quickly, and I believe I learned more from them than they did from me. These inmates were hardly saints, but they certainly had heart and hopefully a future.

During the "Before You Drink, Think Dwight" tour, I would generally make presentations three times a week, sometimes as often as five. When I wasn't speaking, I was preparing a presentation. One day I would appear at a rehab center and speak to a group of thirty people; the next day I would be at a community college speaking to six hundred. My days were busy and satisfying, and I would usually try to do my shopping and other daily chores before or after these speeches. Along the way, I learned that kids have an interesting perspective on people in wheelchairs.

I was doing some food shopping at Piggly Wiggly, a major chain of supermarkets throughout the South, and going about my business without a care in the world. As I was reaching with my gripper for an item on a high self, I felt a jolt at my back and started rolling forward at an extremely fast speed. I tried to slow down by grabbing the wheels, and I looked back to see a young boy pushing me forward just as fast as he could. He was yelling with glee and immersed in the moment before I finally convinced him to stop. The youngster was having a wonderful time pushing my wheelchair as fast it could go, and he thought it was a marvelous toy. He was laughing and enjoying himself—there wasn't a malicious bone in his body. His mother finally caught up with him and was horrified at what at happened. I couldn't help but laugh along with the child, but I did tell him he shouldn't do it again. As much fun as my unexpected journey had been, it was also quite dangerous. Ever since that time, I have learned to keep a sharp lookout for youngsters, and I have stopped more than one intrepid adventurer with similar intents along the way.

By the time I completed my first "Before You Drink, Think Dwight" tour, I had spoken to about 150 organizations and appeared before more than 40,000 people. I had been on television programs and countless radio interviews. It was hard work, and it was uncompensated. Did it make a difference? Like everybody else, I sometimes get discouraged and wonder if it's worth all the effort. Then I get a letter from somebody telling me how I changed their life. Or I get a hug from an inmate. Or I see the huge smile on Mr. Sanford's face in my mind's eye. Yes. This work is worth it. It makes a difference.

13

LEGAL MATTERS

During the four years following the accident in 2005, I had two legal matters to contend with. Posey's criminal trial, and a civil suit I filed to attempt to get compensation for the injuries I suffered from the accident. My attorney, Jon Swartzfager, is a prominent practitioner in Jones County, and he is well known throughout Mississippi. He is a top-notch attorney and has become a close personal friend.

While I was in Forrest General, Mom called Mr. Swartzfager's office based on recommendations from several people who had worked with him. She asked him to visit us in the hospital. I was in a great deal of pain and on many medications when he came by, but I liked him right away.

Mr. Swartzfager's eyes became teary as we spoke, and when we were done, he said, "Dwight, I promise you this. I will do everything in my power to bring you justice and deliver the best possible result we can get. I'll be with you every step of the way." His concern was genuine and his legal skills beyond reproach. I knew I was in good hands.

Herman Posey was a seventy-one-year-old alcoholic who rammed his truck into the rear of my car. He was drunk on the day he hit me, and he had been cited on four prior occasions in recent years for DUI. His license had been revoked and he was driving illegally and without insurance.

Posey was poor, but he managed to post bail and remain free until his trial finally arrived in January 2007. Posey's freedom for more than a year preceding the trial seemed a great injustice and irritant to many in the community, and one of the two stores in Hot Coffee even refused him entrance. He was free all the same to move about the county, work with his lawyer, and plan his legal strategy. Not only that, but he was picked up once again after the accident for driving illegally and for causing a domestic dispute at his neighbor's home while under the influence. I was informed of these occurrences, but I was too focused on my own recovery and physical rehabilitation to concern myself with him. I trusted the state to take care of business.

I wanted to meet Posey at some point before the trial to get a better sense of the man, and I had the opportunity to attend a deposition with Posey and his attorney in preparation for the civil suit. The deposition was scheduled before the criminal trial, so it was my first time seeing him face-to-face. His perspective was immediately apparent when Mr. Swartzfager and I met him that day. He was surly and uncommunicative. When asked about his state of mind and physical condition at the time of the accident, Posey answered, "I wasn't hardly even drunk when the accident happened," as if his legal problems were somehow my fault and a great injustice to him. When he looked at me at all, he showed anger that I was there. The implication was that I had somehow done something wrong by being in his vicinity, and I should have known better. Of course, Posey's blood alcohol level was far in excess of the legal limit at the time of the accident, but by Posey's standards, he was "barely drunk."

Posey showed no concern for having paralyzed me and even implied that I had caused the accident. This shocked me, and it took every ounce of self-control I had not to lunge at him. I did not want to make a scene, however. Tamika had come with me to the deposition, and she was boiling mad, too, but I asked her not to say anything because it would only make matters worse. She held her tongue, but it was probably the hardest thing I'd ever asked her to do. Throughout the deposition and even to this day, Posey has never shown any visible sign of remorse. It was my problem, and I was a nuisance for having gotten in the way.

By the time Posey's criminal trial arrived, I had long before forgiven him. I had been raised with the notion of forgiveness, and I knew that was the path to healing. Vengefulness and hatred wouldn't help me, and I doubted they would make Posey's punishment any worse. The trial lasted only one day, and Posey was convicted of Aggravated DUI. My family and the community at large felt a sense of relief, but the matter of sentencing was still open. I had a role to play in that part of the process.

Everybody seemed to want Posey to never see a day of freedom again. My brothers and other family members wanted me to let the judge know this, but I felt otherwise. I believe in redemption, and while I felt Posey should spend time in jail, I didn't want him to end his days there.

Mr. Swartzfager advised me, "This is your call and only your call, Dwight. Do what your heart tells you to do because you're the one who is going to have to live with it. The judge will likely pay a great deal of attention to your words, and you'll have to live with the results."

I felt that if I acted out of revenge, it would hurt me more than Posey, and with Mr. Swartzfager's help, I wrote a letter to the judge. I explained how my life had changed, the physical pain I had suffered, and the fact that I was confined to a wheelchair for the rest of my life. However, I survived the accident and wanted Posey to have a chance at freedom again before he died. I did not want him to get a sentence that would leave him no hope of outliving his prison term.

I sat in the front row with Mr. Swartzfager during the sentencing phase, and it was clear that the judge wanted to put Posey away for good. He said that Posey represented a threat to the community, showed reckless disregard for the safety of others, and had caused grievous and irreparable injuries to an innocent victim. Posey's actions were part of an ongoing pattern of behavior, and he showed no remorse. However, based on my letter to him, the judge had decided to be as lenient as the law and his conscience would allow. Posey would have to spend at least eight years in jail before becoming eligible for parole. My hope is that he lives long enough to enjoy some freedom in his final days. I felt satisfied with this result and pleased that I had not acted out of anger or resentment. The judge's decision seemed to me to have elements of both justice and forgiveness.

As the sentencing process came to an end, I was startled to see Posey fix his stare upon me. He had avoided looking at me throughout the trial and sentencing, and he now stared at me for about twenty seconds before law enforcement came and put him in handcuffs. I didn't know if his stare was recognition of what he had done to me or hatred for my being on the road that day. Shortly afterwards, however, as Mr. Swartzfager and I were leaving the courthouse, I heard somebody calling my name and hurrying toward me. I did not recognize the man.

"Mr. Owens, I'm Herman's brother. I want you to know just how sorry I am that Herman did this. He deserves his punishment, and I am saddened beyond words for everything you have suffered." I was shocked to hear this but managed to thank him for his concern. I found it ironic that Posey's brother felt so deeply about all of this, but Posey himself could never offer a single word of apology.

With Posey's trial behind us, I felt better able to move forward with the civil suit Mr. Swartzfager was preparing. It was officially filed on August 5, 2008, three years to the day after my accident. Posey, of course, was a defendant, but that was irrelevant. He was in jail and had no assets. Since he was driving illegally and without insurance, we could not proceed against any insurance company. Unfortunately, the person directly responsible for the accident was untouchable.

The second defendant was Chrysler Corporation, and there were several solid reasons to proceed against them. I was driving a 1999 Chrysler Sebring convertible, which bent immediately into a u-shape when the passenger side impacted the tree on the day of the accident. The car was effectively bent in half with me inside.

I was properly strapped in with the seat and shoulder belts firmly buckled, but I was still twisted and spun upside down all the same. Even though Chrysler advertised the Sebring as a safe vehicle with state-of-the-art features to minimize damage in the event of an accident, they had not reinforced the passenger side of the vehicle. Chrysler chose instead to save a few dollars on each vehicle, fully aware that this would result in death or grave injury to a certain percentage of the population. It was a calculated risk on their part, and their calculation was that it would cost less to defend a few lawsuits than to provide this standard safety feature. That decision meant the world to me.

The suit also included theories of false advertising and strict liability for a defective product. The case seemed a likely winner, and we were excited to get the complaint filed and on the docket. Events beyond our anticipation, however, conspired to make the filing useless. On April 30, 2009, Chrysler filed for Chapter 11 bankruptcy protection and petitioned the court to reorganize its debts. The net effect of this was that once the bankruptcy was approved by the Court, Chrysler was able to eliminate many of its prior debts and pending lawsuits, mine among them. Our suit was stopped dead in its tracks and is now a minor footnote in Chrysler's history.

After all was said and done, after well over a million dollars in medical expenses spread over several years, I was left with tens of thousands of dollars in medical bills. I never received a penny in damages from Posey, Chrysler, or any insurance company. The community and my church group, however, stood tall and helped me with fundraisers to pay most of the expenses not covered by my health insurance. At the end of the day, the one thing I know for sure is that the love of a family, an abiding faith in God, and the support of a loving community is a thousand times more important than any monetary compensation I might have received. I received a second chance at life, and that is enough.

14

LIFE GOES ON

The "Before You Drink, Think Dwight" tour wound down toward the middle of 2008. It exceeded my most optimistic hopes. It was fun; it was informative; and it was draining. I closed the tour to take a break from public speaking and to work with other groups that support the disabled community. I also decided to establish a support group called "Men With Disabilities" in my home county of Covington and its surrounding counties in Mississippi.

I have personally counseled hundreds of people with disabilities, and I wanted to put that experience to good use. I have also benefited from the support of these people myself. I chose to limit the group to men because men tend to become less open when there are women in the group. This was nothing against women. I love them. But men are far less likely to talk about the things that concern them most intimately and most profoundly when women are present. These questions generally involve things like:

"Can anybody ever really love me?"
"How can I possibly find a spouse and maintain a loving relationship?"
"I'm having problems sexually. What can I do about it?"

These questions arise all the time, along with a host of other issues about bowel and bladder control in public, not being a burden on your family, dealing with the public at large, and coping with depression and thoughts of suicide. The goal of the group is much more ambitious than just bracing one another to deal with our reality, although that's a big part of it. The broader goal is for us to live our lives boldly and without apology. We want our members to be active in the community, speak and be seen at public events, and become living examples of the worthy and satisfying lives people with disabilities can lead. We urge our members to take a leadership role and educate the public about disabilities. Having a disability doesn't mean having a disabled life.

Our group has people with all kinds of disabilities from blindness or visual impairment to deafness, spinal cord injury, and double amputation.

This may sound like a trailer for a horror show, but the meetings are always upbeat and often quite funny.

"You think you got a sexual problem, Hank? That ain't squat. Here's a problem for you," James offered. And he regaled the group for the next ten minutes with his situation. By the time he was done speaking, there were tears in our eyes and our sides hurt from laughing so much. We could all empathize with James, and we were grateful to hear his story. This kind of experience, however, would never happen in a mixed gathering.

In many ways, my own story is cheerful. Tamika knew me before the accident, suffered through it with me, and she is the most loving wife any man could hope for. Tamika has seen the best and the worst in me, and we have a supportive relationship. We work hard to keep it that way. In the eyes of the men with disabilities I meet, I walk the walk. I am living proof for the non-believer, and while I don't always articulate my story perfectly, the facts of my case bring joy and hope to many others who are wheelchair bound. I drive every day, I go wherever I want, and I am as engaged with the public as any person can be. I love my life, and it shows.

We meet once a month, and the meetings are therapeutic for our spirits and helpful to our community. We talk about events happening in the community, who might appear there, and how we can present our band of brothers in a positive light. We feel better because of our shared circumstances, and we help one another take steps toward becoming an integral part of the community. Everybody wins, and we always have a good time.

I have dealt with many organizations that support the disabled community, and none is better at what they do than Living Independence for Everyone (LIFE). LIFE is staffed for the most part by people with disabilities of every kind, and they know their clientele. They are the boots on the ground helping one person at a time learn to live independently, and their work transforms lives. No matter how severe a person's injury may be, LIFE's goal is to show that person the path to self-reliance and independent living. This means finding apartments that are ADA compliant, obtaining specialized equipment like standing frames, wheelchairs, and scooters, arranging for transportation or Meals on Wheels when necessary, teaching the newly disabled ways to work with their disability, and helping them find jobs. Most important, LIFE brings feelings of self-worth and hope for a better future. LIFE works magic, and I am grateful to have worked with them.

While LIFE's main office is in Jackson, I worked mostly out of their branch in Hattiesburg. I did this almost every day for two years as a Project LINC (Linking Individuals Into Neighborhoods and Communities), AmeriCorps volunteer, and I came to admire the tough love LIFE brings to its mission. While we empathize with people's plights, we focus on the positive. We counsel people one-on-one, not about broad concepts but about how to get specific tasks done. We show newly disabled people that there are others often in worse shape than they are. These people work every day, live in their own homes or apartments, drive wherever they need to go, and build satisfying lives with good careers and loved ones around them. The psychological hurdles are always the toughest, but once people believe in the premise of living independently, then it's just a matter of doing the job. We show them how.

I worked in two primary fields with LIFE. On the technical side, I completed forty-eight ADA audits of businesses in Southern Mississippi using the knowledge of ADA compliance that I had learned from Eddie Jones. I would always call the business first, introduce myself, and let the manager know I was coming by for a site survey. This didn't necessarily fill them with happiness, but it was never adversarial, and many discovered that it's easier to conform to the regulations than they thought. I was not the dreaded presence that many business owners feared, and I would show them specifically how to make easy, low-cost renovations to comply. Typically this involved providing ramp access to a building because wheelchairs can't climb stairs, and perhaps installing grab bars in the bathrooms. I would provide information on how to get this done and then tell them I would be back in forty-five days. Most people wanted to comply and became even more willing when they learned that it's relatively easy. This was an important contribution, but it was not as much fun as the other area where I worked.

The second field of work I enjoyed immensely. I worked on individual cases helping one person at a time gain their independence. My work in this area was effective because I have street credibility in the disabled community. People took one look, and then they listened because they could see my situation. Our disabilities might not be identical, but our challenges were similar no matter what. I could not counsel a blind person on blindness, but I could counsel that person on living independently and insisting upon that right.

A case could last for a week or for several months, and each one was unique. I would handle several at a time. Most cases started out with a person in a desperate situation and often in a depressed or angry state of mind. They usually ended in triumph, with changed circumstances along with a new perspective on the world.

My favorite case was working with Mike, who was twenty years old when we first met. Mike already had a lot of life in the rearview mirror. He had been in the Army, fought and survived in Iraq, and returned home where a drunk driver crashed into the bus he was riding. Mike had escaped the perils of a war zone only to be rewarded with a severed spine when he returned to Mississippi. To my amazement, this didn't seem to dampen his spirit. Mike was irrepressible, and I think I liked him so much because he reminded me of Ryan, my closest friend at rehab, and he made me smile every time we met.

Mike was living in a trailer when I met him, and it was impossible for him to maneuver his wheelchair in the cramped space. He wanted out, but he didn't quite know how to go about it.

"Dwight, I just gotta get my driving certification. I set up my truck with a couple of poles for the brakes and gas. You think that will work?" he asked.

"Mike, don't do that. Are you nuts?" I gasped. "I have a better plan. Let me show you how to drive my truck using a lever for the gas and brakes. Then you'll have a head start when we set you up for driver's training, and it will be a cinch. We can also get your vehicle equipped properly through Vocational Rehab, so you'll be able to afford it all."

I showed Mike how to operate my vehicle, and in a moment of poor judgment, I let him drive the truck for a while with me in the passenger seat. We drove on a quiet country road and didn't go far, but before we could turn off, there was a trail of angry drivers behind us honking because we were going too slowly. It was not my best decision ever, but it filled Mike with a sense of joy and optimism. He saw that he could extend his mobility in the near future, and we quickly made arrangements for him to get his license.

Over the next few months, Mike worked with the VA and purchased a wheelchair-accessible home, and he got his driver's license. He now works actively with young veterans with disabilities and helps bring the same freedom and sense of pride he enjoys to others in similar situations. Cases like Mike's lift my heart, and LIFE has thousands of stories like it. They work tirelessly to bring independence and self-reliance to the newly disabled, and they give them hope for a brighter future.

Not long after I got into the swing of things at LIFE, Tamika's birthday was coming up, and I was thinking hard about a gift for her when she approached me on the topic directly.

"Dwight, I know what you're getting me for my birthday. It's the only thing I want that we don't have. I want a dog," she said.

Rocky had passed recently, and he was really my mom's dog, anyway. I wasn't about to deny Tamika anything in my power to provide, so we started asking around and scanning the newspapers and Internet for a Yorkie pup. These are high-spirited, family dogs, and that's what Tamika wanted.

We went to visit a breeder to see the new litter of Yorkies pups she had available, and Tamika fell in love. She selected Maxi at first sight, and Maxi has run the household ever since. She is smart, sassy, and nothing but love. She sleeps under my wheelchair, but after I ran over her one time by accident, she learned to listen for any motion I might make. We are both more careful now.

Since Tamika is now a guidance counselor and is usually at school, Maxi and I spend a lot of time at home together. She has learned what car keys are, and she stares at me suspiciously whenever she sees them in my hands. Maxi loves to make a break for it, and on several occasions, she has scooted out the door before I could catch her. I have had to roll myself a quarter of a mile to my grandmother's home up the road to pick Maxi up after she escaped for an adventure. I now take extraordinary precautions and lock her in the garage before I go out. She moans her protest as I leave and then snubs me when I get back until I make it up to her with an extra long scratch or a treat of some kind. And like Rocky, Maxi knows the sound of Tamika's car. She runs to the door with her butt wiggling a mile a minute before Tamika enters, and she acts as if Tamika had been gone for a month. On numerous occasions, Tamika has commented, "Dwight, you could learn a lot about greeting people from Maxi. Plus, she always gets rewarded with a good scratch. Hmmm."

I worked with the Project LINC full time for two years and was in their Jackson headquarters one day when my supervisor, Margie Moore, the Director of Project LINC for AmeriCorps, told me, "Dwight, I've nominated you for the National Service Award. Not only for your remarkable work with LIFE, but also for your support group and all the public speaking you've done as well. You can light up a room, and I want you to know how much I appreciate everything you do."

I was stunned by Ms. Moore's comments, and I was honored.

"Now, don't get your hopes up," she went on. "They only select three winners, and there are several thousand nominations. I think you're that special, but that doesn't mean you'll get the award."

I understood completely, but I was still walking on air because she thought enough of me to go through the drill and submit the nomination. It was no small chore, and the odds of my being selected were long.

I received a call from Margie in February of 2010.

"Dwight we got it!" she exclaimed. "We got it. You won. Out of the thousands of nominees, they chose you for the National Service Award. I'm going to New York to watch you get the award," she added. "I wouldn't miss it for the world."

I was in shock. I knew what many of the other nominees had accomplished, and I never expected this result. I was grateful to be mentioned in the same breath as some of these other people, but I did not give myself the slightest chance of winning. My heart was beating out of my chest, and I couldn't believe my good fortune.

There were two other Spirit of Service award winners in 2010. One was retired Army Colonel Gary LaGrange. After retiring from active duty, Gary established a charity called "Help Us Learn, Give Us Hope." He worked sixty hours a week developing contacts, meeting with suppliers, and providing the logistical know-how to help school children in war-torn Iraq and Afghanistan. Over the past few years, Gary's organization has delivered more than 520,000 pounds of school supplies along with 40,000 schoolbooks to children in these countries. His efforts now extend to Africa and the Balkans. Gary is a remarkable tale of ingenuity, hard work, and persistence. He has partnered with the US military to bring hope and better lives to thousands of youngsters.

The other award winner was Janice Klein-Young, who has spent the last thirty-six years teaching fine arts in the roughest school district in Miami. Her school is the last chance for kids who have been expelled from their regular schools, and she deals every day with challenges that most people would flee. Ninety percent of her students have been in jail already, and most come from broken homes or worse. None of this fazes Janice, and she puts the kids to work. After they have learned a set of skills, she takes them to nursing homes, rehab centers, and even juvenile detention centers. The kids then become the instructors and teach the skills they recently learned to their own students. For many of these kids, this is the first time in their lives that they have been looked to with respect and admiration. It's a life-changing experience, and the graduation rate at Janice's school is remarkable considering where these kids were starting from when they first reached her. Gary and Janice are two amazing people with even more amazing stories. I felt like I was the old workhorse in a stable full of Kentucky Derby winners.

The National Service Award ceremonies were held at Radio City Music Hall in Manhattan for three days in June 2010, and the three Spirit of Service award winners were treated like royalty. We had our pictures on a huge neon display outside Rockefeller Center, and they dominated the landscape. Tamika was beaming with pride through all this; she did everything she could to absorb the moment. The event was hosted in large part by Al Roker, the television personality. Governor Paterson, Mayor Bloomberg, senators, congresspeople, and many media celebrities were everywhere. Michelle Obama had attended the 2009 event but could not be there in 2010. Instead, she provided a videotaped message to the audience. And as a football player in my earlier days, I was happy to meet Erik Ainge, the backup quarterback for the New York Jets at the time. We had lunch at Gracie Mansion, the mayor's home, and enjoyed two evening galas. Media coverage was constant, and through the frenzy of it all, I had the good fortune of meeting a remarkable lady named Roberta MacDonald. True to form, Roberta appeared out of nowhere and introduced herself by walking up and kissing me on the cheek.

Roberta is the Director of Marketing for Cabot Creamery Cooperative based in Vermont, and she believes the best marketing strategy for Cabot is to support communities. She does not fill the airwaves with more noise or jingles, nor does she have dancing leprechauns clamoring on about Cabot's cheese and dairy products. Instead, she directs Cabot's marketing dollars toward public works. For example, she directed the Great American Voter Trek in 2008, in which a group of Cabot-sponsored cyclists biked across much of the country promoting voter registration events at major cities. This non-partisan adventure took on a life of its own, and it captured the public's attention. In another instance, Cabot sponsored the Put A Bad Beat On Hunger poker tournament at Borgata Casino in Atlantic City. Cabot arranged for major poker celebrities to participate in the charitable event and helped raise funds for New Jersey food banks.

"Dwight, we're sponsoring a celebrity cruise for hometown heroes across the country, and you and Tamika have to join us," she said. Roberta gets right to the point, and I liked her immediately. I smiled and said I'd be delighted to be a part of it—not quite knowing what "it" was all about.

It turns out that Cabot has sponsored a cruise program for the past two years to recognize the contributions of various volunteers across the country. They get radio stations from Maine to Florida to promote the event, review nominations, and select winners from their regions. The winners are all people who volunteer big doses of their time, energy, and ingenuity to local causes without any thought of personal reward. Cabot arranges round-trip travel from their homes to Miami, where the ship departs from, and then a group of over one hundred people enjoys a week-long Caribbean cruise together. The more I learned, the more I looked forward to being part of this group. Plus, who wouldn't enjoy a Caribbean cruise?

The coming year, 2011, was already shaping up to be one for the books. I had met Jonathan Praet, and we were making plans to write this book. I had plans to start a second "Before You Drink, Think Dwight" tour. I was going on a cruise, courtesy of Cabot, which would be the honeymoon Tamika and I had postponed for the past three years. Yes, life was good, and Tamika and I loved every minute of it.

15

DÉJÀ VU

As 2010 was winding down, everything seemed to be in its proper place. The book was coming along at a brisk clip. Every day with Tamika was a good day, and we were getting ready for a cruise in January. I was working on computers for some friends, giving periodic presentations, and tutoring kids in the community. Life was good, and I was filling my days with things that mattered to me. Then I got the call.

"Dwight, it's Eric. Greg's been in a terrible accident. We don't know how bad he's hurt, but he's been flung about thirty feet from his car. I'm on the scene, and we're calling for a helicopter to medevac him to Forrest General."

My mother had gotten remarried a few years earlier, and Eric is my stepfather. He's a great guy and a welcome addition to the family. He's also a volunteer on the Hot Coffee Fire Department, and he was one of the first people called to the accident. It was two o'clock in the morning on October 23, 2010.

Tamika and I rushed to get dressed and go to the hospital. We drove by the scene of the accident on the way and saw that Greg's car had flipped over and was charred black by fire. We saw a large stain of blood on the road and feared the worst. We had made the trek to Forrest General too many times in the past, and we drove in silence, each afraid to speak. We knew Greg was in bad shape, but we were in shock to hear Eric's report when we arrived.

"Greg's in the Emergency Room right now. The road is real curvy where he had the accident, and we think he was probably driving too fast, lost control of the car, and it flipped. Greg was hurled almost thirty feet away from the vehicle, which may have saved his life. The car caught fire and exploded while I was there. Greg would never have survived if he was inside."

Greg is my cousin, but he's more like a brother to me. He spent much of his youth living with us; he went to school with me every day; and we were in the same grade together. Greg is also the person who helped me every day during my months of home rehab. He would set me up on the motorized bike to exercise my legs; he would spot me as I worked in my standing frame; and he would check on my physical and mental health every day. I love Greg dearly, and I was deeply afraid for him.

As the hours passed, we saw medical staff entering and leaving Greg's room. We heard him yell in pain—but we were actually encouraged by that. We knew he was alive and could feel pain. Pain passes, and we were glad to hear his moans. By the time Greg was stabilized, there were about thirty friends and family in the waiting room. The attending physician came out around seven in the morning and invited us all to a conference room so he could give us an update.

"Greg is stabilized," he said, "but he's had several serious injuries. He has broken ribs and a punctured lung. But there's something much worse. Greg severed his spinal cord at T-5 and will be paralyzed for the rest of his life. He will need your help, love, and patience for a long, long time."

There was a gasp in the room when we heard these last words, and Tamika whispered, "My Lord, not again."

We were stunned, and tears rolled down my cheeks. It seemed cruel and unfair. The four of us boys, Cedrick, Voncarie, Greg, and I grew up together and felt a bond none of us can fully explain. Two of the four were now confined to wheelchairs for the rest of our lives, both of us having met this fate long before our thirtieth year. It was more than I could bear, and I rolled away to sit by myself and try to make sense of it all.

For all the joys life brings, it can also be unbearably harsh. I knew what lay ahead for Greg, and the knowing made it harder for me, not easier. This seemed a malicious twist of fate for Greg, me, and my family. What had we done to deserve this?

I visited Greg at the hospital every day for the next several weeks and watched as he went through the same stages of denial and anger that everyone in his situation experiences. I had a trove of knowledge that could help him, but I knew he wasn't ready yet. Nor was the family. This felt like a bad dream we had all been through before. The whole family would have to commit to Greg's recovery; it would take time, patience, and many loving hearts to restore Greg's self-confidence and will to live. Above all, it would require every drop of courage and perseverance Greg could muster to understand in his heart that he still had a full and productive life ahead of him.

Greg had to learn to accept his new circumstances, but we all needed time. Time, patience, and love. This would be a long journey, and Greg would somehow have to find a way to take one breath after the other and build a future from the wreckage of the accident. He would have to learn to forgive himself; he would have to experience the physical pain and learn to relish all the small triumphs of rehabilitation; he would have to come to terms with God; and he would need the support and love of the family every step of the way.

I had to immerse myself in something positive after Greg's accident; otherwise I felt like I might explode. I worked on this book hour after hour; I completed interviews several times a week; I researched old notes; and I just tried to keep moving forward. I felt numb. I met Greg with a smile every day, but he could sense my despair. I knew what he was going through, and I would do everything I could to ease his path. It would not be easy for me. It would be brutal for Greg.

As 2010 came to an end, Tamika and I made preparations to join the Cabot Creamery staff and their guests on the Cabot Celebrity Cruise. This was the perfect medicine for Tamika and me. It came at the time we needed it most, and it helped us focus on something positive. It gave us something to look forward to, and it turned out to be everything we hoped for and more.

My two friends from the National Service Award, Gary LaGrange and Janice Klein-Young, were there along with thirty-six other cruise winners from around the country. We luxuriated in the Caribbean for a week; we dined lavishly; we were nourished by the companionship of our fellow travelers; and we let the cares of the world roll off our backs. It was glorious and self-indulgent. It was uplifting and inspiring. Mostly, it was restorative.

I was inspired by the remarkable accomplishments of my fellow travelers and the challenges they had overcome to make a difference. They had formed local groups that donated time and funds to the neediest in their communities; they had established foundations that earned national recognition; they had served as volunteer EMTs for decades; they were teachers, nurses, writers, moms and dads. Above all, they were living proof that one person willing to put heart and soul into something can do extraordinary things for their community. I came to love these people, and they are a constant source of inspiration to me. They make me humble, and they prod me into action when I might otherwise let things slide.

After the cruise, I had a lengthy conversation with Tamika, and we decided to undertake a second "Before You Drink, Think Dwight" tour. I reached out to contacts in Mississippi and neighboring states, held a thirty-minute interview on Clear Channel Radio that ran several times on numerous stations in the state, and started to plan out the next six months of speaking engagements. I am energized. I am focused. And I brace myself with the thought that when I do this tour the next time, Greg will be at my side as a fellow speaker.

As this phase of my life draws to a close, I look back and see a different person in my past. Before the accident, I had never given a thought to the disabled community. It's not that I didn't care; there just wasn't time. It wasn't part of my experience. I was young, full of energy, and busy chasing my dreams. I was dealing with the press of day-to-day affairs and loving life… when all my plans and dreams were stopped dead in their tracks. Posey crashed into my car while in a drunken stupor, and my life's trajectory veered into a direction I could never have imagined.

I have learned many things along the way. I have learned humility and found the strength to graciously accept the help of friends and family who give so much with loving and open hearts. I have learned the healing power of forgiveness, and I bear Posey no ill will. I have seen the joy of others as they shared in each small success I achieved in my recovery. I have come to trust God and know that He has a plan for me. And I have become what I always wanted to be. A teacher. I share my story and gratefully, gently inform the able-bodied world about the disabled community. I try to use my life as proof for people with disabilities that they can have a wonderful life ahead of them. I try to offer hope.

I have grown and learned much. I have learned in my heart that there is nothing more powerful or enriching than the love of family and community. I have learned also that I and my fellow travelers in the disabled community have much to offer. It is up to us to live our lives boldly and without apology. We are proof to the world that there is no challenge the human spirit cannot overcome.

My name is Dwight Owens. This is the beginning of my story.

EPILOGUE

I spent countless hours with Jonathan Praet, my author and now my dear friend, recounting my story in fractured bits and pieces. He worked with me and labored over every word to put this story into my voice. His endless and sometimes annoying questions forced me to review my life at a level of detail that few people ever do.

At first it seemed too early to write this personal tale. So much lies ahead. I thought, "I'll just do this later when I have more to say." But plans like this tend to fade into distant memory and get lost in the press of day-to-day affairs. I had my story, and I had my author. I had to share my journey.

This has been a labor of love. I truly believe that "to whom much is given, much is expected." I have received gifts beyond measure in my life, and this short book is a way to thank my family, my church, my community, and my God for their unfailing faith and support. And although the book is short, my goals are grand.

People with disabilities fight more than their physical traumas. They battle depression and forces that can make them feel useless. They battle loss of pride and independence, and they battle self-speak that can lead to suicide. They battle stares and glares from the world, and they harbor hidden thoughts that make them wonder if they should continue the battle at all. I see this every day. I know it in my soul. I'm here to say they should.

My goal is to help lift the spirits of people with disabilities and to be an example to the world at large by proving that a disability is just a setback, not a life sentence. My goal is to show the world at large that people with disabilities are people above all else. We, the disabled, have spirits and minds to compete with the best in the world. I know this from my life experience, and it is an unassailable truth. I often tell people I can do everything they can do, I just do it sitting down. To my fellow travelers with disabilities, I say this: "Rock on. There's nothing you can't accomplish."

Dwight Owens
December 2011

IN MEMORIAM

My cousin Gregory passed away on October 24, 2011, one year and two days after the tragic accident that severed his spinal cord. Gregory's death was sudden and unexpected. He was 29 years old.

Gregory grew up with me and my family. He attended school with my brothers and me, he played sports with us, and he helped me every day with my home health care after returning from physical rehabilitation in Jackson. His accident struck the very soul of our family following so quickly on the heels of my own. During this past year, Gregory experienced the full range of physical and emotional upheaval that comes from such a horrific, life-changing event. He was depressed. He wondered why the use of his body had been cut in half. He was angry. And then he accepted his condition. He became confident and even exuberant at times at what his future may hold. We talked about Gregory appearing with me on the speaking circuit, about continuing his rehab, and about his future.

I spoke with Gregory the day he died. He was filled with excitement about learning how to drive again and getting his license. Things were looking up. There was laughter in his voice and confidence about the road ahead. That night, with his heart filled with hope and his spirit eager to face the future, he died. Abruptly and with no warning. We don't know why. We just trust.

There is a gaping void in the heart and in the soul of my family. We grew up with Gregory. We teased him. We cried with him. We shared our lives with him. Now we mourn him. All we know for sure is that we loved him, and we will miss him forever.

Dwight Owens
October 2011

The Wedding

The Reception

A New Addltion

Dwight and Tamika's beautiful daughter, Brailey Samara Owens, was born on 12/12/12 after the 1st edition of "Stll Standing" was published in 2011.

Moving Forward

"Dwight's motivational speaking and service has been sought after throughout Mississippi and beyond."

SPECIAL THANKS

Dwight and Jonathan Praet extend their profound gratitude to the many people who played such an integral role in bringing this book to print.

- Our good friends at Cabot Creamery Cooperative for their critical help in editing and publishing this work.

- Joy Clark and Laurel Barbieri for their constant encouragement and in-depth, insightful, and sometimes sharp-elbowed commentary on the writing.

- Eric Levy for his comprehensive edit and unwavering insistence that we "publish this book now."

- The Mississippi Department of Rehabilitation Services for their dedication as the state agency in helping Mississippians with disabilities live and work independently.

More people than we can name deserve our thanks and recognition for their support of this project. Among them are:

- Lesa and Eric Clark
- James and Sally Moffett
- Pastor Evans and New Hopewell Missionary Baptist Church
- Pastor Hanchey and Christ's Church
- Chinika Hughes
- Jessica Chandler
- Chris Blount
- Dr. Duncan Donald
- Miriam and Kenneth Schrock
- Dwight's extended family
- LIFE of Mississippi
- MS Department of Rehabilitation Services
- Evelyn & Mike Kormanik
- Staten Island Giving Circle

Finally, Tamika Owens, Dwight's wife, was an inspiration, source of strength, and tireless contributor to this book. Without her help and encouragement, it would not have happened.

Made in the USA
Monee, IL
20 March 2022

93104610R00083